# THE
# PRINCIPLES OF
# HEALING

*By*

## H. B. JEFFERY

**Published and for sale by**

CHRIST TRUTH LEAGUE

2400 Canton Drive

Fort Worth, Texas 76112

Other Books

By Author

CHRISTIANITY (paper)

COORDINATION of SPIRIT, SOUL, and BODY

The FRUIT of the SPIRIT (paper)

The LORD'S PRAYER (paper)

MYSTICAL TEACHINGS

The SPIRIT of PRAYER

THREE TREATMENTS (paper)
(Prosperity, Healing, Transcendent)

The POWER of the NAME

H. B. Jeffery

## GREETINGS!

TO my many friends and students in America, and across the seas: May you walk always with the Saviour's love in the presence of God; ever listening, and ever following Him who is the Spirit of Truth. For Christ said unto you,

> *Blessed are they that hear the word*
> *of God, and keep it.*
> *If ye know these things, happy are ye*
> *if ye do them.*

H. B. J.

# CONTENTS

PAGE.

# THE PRINCIPLES OF HEALING

## LESSON I

THERE is probably nothing in our ministry of the Truth that appeals to the people so much as the subject of healing. All the people in the world seem to need healing; and many of them are now turning to the ministration of the Spirit, rather than to man-made methods of treatment.

More than ever before, people are seeking for that vital and essential knowledge of the Truth which shall free them from the sorrow, sickness, and death they have so mistakenly believed in as an unavoidable part of life.

In our study of the principles of healing, whether as beginners or as experienced practitioners, we may increase our knowledge of Christian healing by glancing first at some of the references to the healing art which have come down to us through history.

For there have always been some forms of mental or spiritual healing practiced in the world, and we have many records of men in distress who were thus delivered from their afflictions. It is also noticeable that the ills which troubled mankind centuries ago are the same ills which people are prone to give their attention to now.

The practice of healing is not a new art, but was studied and known in former times; and there were many methods and many schools of healing, psychical schools and spiritual schools. As far back as we can look, we find that men were divided in regard to methods of healing and also in regard to the meaning of disease.

Among the early Hebrews, disease was looked upon as the result of "sin." It was thought that if there were anything troubling a person, it was due to the fact that, consciously or unconsciously, he had disobeyed some law of being; in other words, he had "sinned." So it became a part of the office of the High Priest to heal disease by bringing the sin to light and erasing it.

The ancient Hebrews believed so entirely in this relationship between sin and disease that the High Priest would not enter the Holy of Holies if he discovered in himself any disturbance of mind or body. If there were the least blemish on his flesh, he considered himself unworthy to approach the Inner Sanctuary.

Sickness was considered a disturbance of a man's spirit or a disturbed relation between a man and his Maker, and it was believed that every form of disease was due to this inner disturbance. All sicknesses and diseases were the outcome of sin, which was a state of disobedience by which man had violated his sacred trust as a son of the Supreme Being and for which he was suffering.

There was the same thought among the ancient Greeks. If a man found himself in a condition of illness, he sought the priest as an intercessor for him with that god who was supposed to have the healing power.

In fact, among all the civilized and half-civilized peoples of ancient times, we find that sickness was looked upon as the result of sin, which was a disturbance in man's spirit

by its self-separation from the Divine Spirit. So men so-
licited the office of their high priest that they might be
restored to their right relation with their God or gods.

Nevertheless, as man's curiosity was always proceeding
outward toward his world, the belief in material remedies
arose in his mind. For, according to appearances, man was
a material being, a kind of human animal which was no
different from other animals except that, unlike other animals, man had a mysterious something which he called
his "soul."

The common belief of modern man is much the same today. People speak of the "human animal." They believe
that mankind is subject to a material life which is governed by material laws. They think that their diseases are
physical, and that the remedy for them is to be obtained
by administering the compounds of matter to the outer
man. So there has grown up the widespread, apparently
reasonable doctrine of *materia medica* which says that disease is material and that the remedy for it is to be found
in matter.

But let us turn back to ancient Greece; for in that country, in the Fifth Century B. C., there was a school of thought
which maintained that there is in man a ruling Spirit,
called the *Psyche,* or "Breath." Socrates was the founder
of this school of thought. He taught that the *Psyche* is
immortal, that it is the Essential of life.

We remember that this same recognition of the Breath
was the foundation of the ancient Hebrew belief, as when
Elihu said to Job: "The Spirit of God hath made me, and

the Breath of the Almighty hath given me life." The word *breath*, the word *spirit*, and the word *psyche* have the same meaning; they refer to the One Essential.

Socrates urged men to tend to their *Psyche*, to make it as good as possible. Modern psychology claims that most of man's sickness of mind and body is due to a perturbation of the *psychical*. The psychologists have borrowed the word *psyche* from the Greeks. It is often equated with the *soul*.

But most people do not know what is meant by the word *soul*. Their idea of such a thing is vague and confused, although they may believe that there is something in man which cannot be disturbed without affecting his mind and body. It is the consciousness.

Jesus came into this world (about 500 years after Socrates) to express the same principle that Socrates had believed in. We find that His teachings are quite in accord with those of Socrates.

Nevertheless there was this great difference: Jesus not only believed in the Principle of Life, but He *was* It. Socrates, on the other hand, although he believed in the Good as the All, could not rise above the test he was put to and went down to his death. When he drank the hemlock he was poisoned and passed out. His teaching was quite correct, but he could not feel and know as Jesus did: *I Am It*.

The teachings of Jesus are like those of Socrates in that they both believed that man is an immortal spiritual being. But Jesus was fully aware of the Truth that He was the Son of the Divine Being. He knew that, if God is Spirit, the Son of God must be Spirit in his Real Nature.

Socrates did not embody the theory; Jesus Christ did. As Paul said, Jesus was the "fulness of the Godhead"; He had within Him "all the treasures of wisdom and knowledge." With the Divine Wisdom and Knowledge, Jesus could prove that what He said was true—and He did so.

"All power hath been given unto Me in heaven and in earth."

"All things that the Father hath are Mine."

"I and My Father are one."

"He that hath seen Me hath seen the Father."

"I lay down My life that I might take it again. . . . I have power to lay it down, and I have power to take it again."

Jesus not only said these things, but He proved them. He was the conscious embodiment of the Principle that man is Spirit, that he is the son of God, that he is a divine being, the child of the Most High, in no way material and therefore not governed by material law.

We speak of "material law," but when we do so we must remember that there is no such thing. So-called matter and material law are merely man's surface judgment of things as they appear. Man has erred in his discernment and therefore in his judgment. But the righteous judgment of Jesus is living proof of the Principle that God is All in All. God is not material. God is Spirit.

Science is now rapidly coming to this conclusion, at least in theory; for the more far-seeing of our modern scientists are saying that our universe is a spiritual universe, that there is no such thing as matter. They are already trying to prove to the world that so-called "matter" and Spirit are one.

When these advanced physicists have delved deep enough, they will find it to be true scientifically that there are not, and never were, two substances. And when they are fully convinced that there is only one substance, they will perceive that this one substance is not material but spiritual —of the Spirit.

They will then acknowledge that God is All in all, and that beside Him there is none else. Indeed, there is already one recognized scientist of the first rank who has boldly stated that the entire universe is nothing but God.

In the course of scientific discovery, it will be seen that man is not only essentially spirit, but is totally a spiritual being: not mortal but immortal; and being immortal, not governed by mortal laws.

Man is governed by God, Who is Spirit. Therefore, whatever he may think to the contrary, he is not subject to material conditions but can rise above them by his knowledge of the Divine Law of Spirit. As man perceives and understands the Truth of Being, he ascends to that high level of consciousness wherein he can feel the Oneness and Allness of God, and see that there is no other being but God.

Man can realize within himself and know the truth that was declared by the Spirit through the ancient prophets:

"Do not I fill heaven and earth? saith the Lord."

"The heaven is My throne, and the earth is My footstool."

"Look unto Me, and be ye saved, all the ends of the earth: for I am God, and there is none else."

"All the earth shall be filled with the glory of the Lord."
This is the state of consciousness to which we must ascend
if we are to be the high form of Being that Jesus was, and
therefore heal as He did: by the Divine Presence, without
any effort or struggle or strain or so-called "treatment."

As healers, we are witnesses and thus vehicles of the
Truth. We do not treat or try to work the Law of Being.
The Law of the Spirit of Life works by its own power in
and through man. As we keep watch in the Spirit of Truth,
we know that it is the Spirit of God Himself which is All in
all to wield and to do His Law.

In Christ we find that Law to be an actual dynamic force,
right now, within us and all about us, with nothing to op-
pose it. There is no other power or presence or force or
intelligence save the One. If we can lift our minds wholly
to that One, we shall be healing even as Jesus healed; for
Jesus said, "He that believeth on Me, the works that I do
shall he do also; and greater works than these shall he do."
We shall do those works, if we know the Truth.

Our problem of healing lies simply in our knowing the
Truth, in our realization of the Truth. We must become
conscious of the Fact that God is All, and that there is no
other presence or power or substance or intelligence. We
must know that there is no other being but God — the One
and Only, Whose Glory is round about us.

We walk in His Glory and are surrounded by it. It fills
not only our environment but also ourselves. We are children of His Glory; we were born to it. We are children of
Light and not of darkness, of Day and not of night, of the
Free Spirit and not of flesh. We are in the Divine Presence

constantly and are never absent from God because He is ever present.

The Spirit is omnipresent, and it is quite impossible for us to absent ourselves from Its Presence. We could not, even if we would. We live and move and have our being in God, and He works in us to will and to do of His good pleasure. Jesus told us that it is the "Father's good pleasure" to give us the Kingdom.

We know that the Kingdom of God is already within us now. We are the sons of God now. We are at one with God now. This is the consciousness to which we must ascend and in which we must live, if we are to do that work which Jesus said it would be our privilege to do — that same work which He did, and in the manner in which He did it.

For this work we must strengthen our consciousness by raising it to higher levels of realization. We must abide in the Divine Consciousness, and walk in it steadfastly and habitually. For we must be *living* agencies of God in order to carry on the healing work.

Healing, after all, is incidental to consciousness. We need not stress it so much as we sometimes do. If we are in the right state of consciousness, we do the work without effort and without any form of personal responsibility. We work almost automatically.

The Divine Principle of Truth has its own power and law and *modus operandi*. It works through us while we are simply abiding in the Truth and walking in the consciousness of the Presence. In the true consciousness we find that the Power which "worketh righteousness" is the *only and ever present Power.*

Jesus knew that there is but the One Presence and Power, and that It does the work. He knew and acknowledged that the work was already done, because that One Presence and Power can see no evil and can perceive no illness. He spoke the word of Truth by knowing it. So he who would heal, paradoxical as this may seem, must be he who sees nothing to heal and therefore makes no effort to heal.

If you watch carefully what Jesus did in healing, you will notice that He made no effort to heal; that, in fact, He did supremely nothing. They brought to Him those that were ill, and they got well. They brought to Him the blind and the maimed, and in His Presence these conditions departed; they were gone. We have no record indicating that He diagnosed cases or inquired into the history of them. He did not take temperatures or ask about symptoms or look at tongues. He did not feel pulses; He made no physical examination; but people got well immediately. It is written that all manner of sickness and disease was healed by Him.

The sickness of the people whom Jesus healed was solely in the realm of appearance. They appeared to be ill, and they appeared to be well. All such appearances are in the world of phenomena and are made of illusion. Jesus knew the non-reality of the material world, and He knew that the essential nature of man is God. He knew of that Spirit in man that "worketh righteousness." "There is a Spirit in man: and the inspiration of the Almighty giveth them understanding."

Jesus was aware of that Spirit, conscious of it, alive to it. He knew that the Spirit is the only Being, Substance, Intelligence. He always turned to that Spirit and away from appearances. His words, "Judge not according to the appearance," mean: Do not be disturbed by appearances; do not let your judgment be formed by that which your senses report to you, because your senses are betrayers and false witnesses; they tell you that which is not so. *Judge not by appearances.*

You may notice that when they brought a paralytic to Jesus, He did not concern Himself with the case. He was not anxious. He merely said, "Arise, take up thy bed, and go unto thine house." In the same way He was unconcerned with the withered arms and the lunacies and the fevers and all the various afflictions that seemed to have fastened themselves upon men and women. He was not interested in diseases. He was not a student of pathology, of hygiene, or of anatomy. Yet He was not ignorant of the physical body, nor of the diverse theories and practices that men think so important to human welfare.

Jesus had the eye which could penetrate through so-called matter. He had the discernment which could know the thoughts and feelings of men. His eye was not governed by material law, nor was He deceived by any sense of matter with its supposed solidity and resistance. He could see that what is called matter is only the outer picture of men's thoughts and beliefs.

Jesus was not governed by time or space, nor was He in any way bound by the limited states of mind under which most men labor. He was a free Being because He was not controlled by His senses and not deluded by the law of matter, but was governed by the Law of the Spirit of Life.

He said, "It is the Spirit that giveth life; the flesh profiteth nothing."

Jesus transcended man's senses; and never judging by what the outer eye perceived or the outer ear reported, He judged righteous judgment and beheld Reality. He was wholly conscious of the Reality and was therefore not in the least troubled by appearances. They brought to Him all manner of sickness, probably every known form of disease, but He did not catalogue them in His mind. He did not look upon some as curable and others as incurable. He in no way judged by the appearances that were presented to Him, but continued to judge righteous judgment, saying, as it were:

"Know ye not that ye are the children of God, the offspring of the Most High? Ye are divine beings, hidden by these appearances which ye have thought to be your life. But these conditions, these appearances, which seem to be so real, are not real. They are false conceptions, false beliefs, and there is no truth in them. They have no place in the Mind of God. Your Heavenly Father does not see you that way. His Eye is too pure to behold iniquity."

We are spoken of in the Scripture as "lights." "Ye are the light of the world." The scientists of today are now telling us that the universe is a universe of light. Such men as are of the caliber of Sir James Jeans, although they have worked as physicists and materialists, are now seeing beyond the confines of the seeming laws of matter, and are telling us that all is life and light.

He who would do good healing must walk in the consciousness of that Light within himself. He must be consciously a child of the Heavenly Father in Whom there is no shadow. He must know that he is the son of God. The sun is a shining, radiant being; and that is the meaning of the word "son" when we are said to be the "sons of God." In our sonship to God we are truly radiant with the Light of the Father.

Therefore, walk in the Master's footsteps with an eye that is single, for He said, "If thine eye be single, thy whole body shall be full of light." Then shall you see the universal Light, because it is by the Light which is within you that you see the Light which is roundabout you. Also, when you are conscious of that inward Light, you will be conscious of it in your fellow men. You will be aware of the presence of that Light within others, even as within yourself.

The Spirit of life is the Spirit of understanding and of knowledge and of wisdom. Wisdom is light. We speak of one who is intelligent as being one who is "enlightened." Such an one is imbued with light. When a man understands a subject he can throw light upon it. Understanding is light. God is Understanding. God is Light. God is Wisdom.

Man, therefore, is a child of Wisdom, not of ignorance. He is not a foolish being, an idiot, an ignoramus. He·is a child of Light. The Spirit of the Father is that "true Light, which lighteth every man that cometh into the world."

The healer must know the Presence of Light. He must work in the consciousness of the Light; he must be aware of it, must walk in that true state of being wherein he shall find no necessity for struggling and straining to heal. Healing is done under the action of Light.

When Jesus went about healing all manner of sickness

and disease, He did not labor to do physical things, nor did He treat any physical conditions. He did not say that He was concerned about the people or their conditions, and yet He went about doing good. Good was done wherever He moved. Wherever He went something good appeared. He did nothing to make it happen; it just took place. People were healed, not by what He did, but by what He was. He was the Fullness of the Divine Light, and His consciousness of oneness with "the Father of lights" was what did the work; for the principle of the whole universe is one of consciousness.

Our modern scientists are now telling us that the whole universe is consciousness. They have resolved it back to consciousness. In their research, their insight has transcended matter and material law, transcended even life, and has touched the fact that the universe is pure consciousness. This is quite in accord with the statements of the ancient prophets who declared that God is Infinite Force or Consciousness, the One and Only Presence, Power, and Intelligence.

Jesus, who was fully aware of that Truth and walked in His awareness of it, could see that man is simply a being of consciousness. His healing was done because He walked in the true Consciousness, knowing that there is but That One Consciousness. He had the Divine Consciousness in Himself and knew that it is the All-consciousness. And so, living and walking in that Consciousness, and knowing that He was luminous and full of Light, there was healing in His Presence.

Jesus did not do things. Things were done by the Presence and Power of that Light, that Wisdom, that Consciousness, in which He knew Himself to be immersed. He was baptized, or saturated, with it; for the word "baptize" means to saturate or soak. Jesus was saturated with the Consciousness of the Oneness and Allness of God. He knew the Truth and walked in it, and that was His Power to do the work.

"Ye shall know the Truth, and the Truth shall make you free." The Truth is dynamic. The Truth never slumbers, but is ever active. It works only through those who are conscious of it, who know the Allness of it, and who walk in the realization of it.

If you can walk in that pure state of consciousness, if you can "let this Mind be in you, which was also in Christ Jesus," you will do the things that Jesus did.

In the true state of mind we can work without effort or strain, and without any sense of there being anything to heal. The healing will take place because we are dwelling in the realization of the Truth. The Truth will act because of its own law, and we may not even be aware that anything is being done.

It is undoubtedly in this manner that Jesus healed: not by giving attention to the cases, not by studying or inquiring or diagnosing, but by moving freely in the realization of the Oneness of God. Those who came into His Presence received something of that realization and felt the stirring of the Life Principle within themselves. As they were awakened, Life welled up in them and they felt themselves restored, renewed, made whole.

Not by any conscious effort of the human man, but by

the active Principle of the Divine Spirit in which He lived and moved and had His being, did Christ work. This is the state of consciousness that we should have, and must have, if we would do the work as Jesus Christ did it — and said we could do it.

People say that Jesus lived long ago. They say that He was the Son of God, that He had the power from on High, but that the days of miracles have passed, that Jesus is gone, and we live in another time and a different age. But to this we must reply:

" 'I am the Lord. I change not.' From everlasting to everlasting, God is God; and the Kingdom of God is from everlasting to everlasting, without beginning or end. It is not variable, nor is it touched by shadow cast by turning. There is no past, present, or future. There is no past age of miracles; neither is there a Golden Age to come. *Now* God is, and *now* is His Kingdom, and *now* are we the sons of God."

The healer must dwell always in that consciousness of NOW, knowing that there is no past to regret and no future to dread. There is no past; there is no future; there is only I AM.

We dwell in the Presence of the Living God. We cannot live yesterday or tomorrow. We can only live now. God is I AM, and I AM is now. We dwell, now and here, in the Realization which God has of Himself. That perfect Self-knowledge is I AM. We dwell in the Perfection of God, in the Truth and the Goodness and the Purity and the Sweetness and the Power and the dynamic Energy and Life of God, who IS, and whose Name is I AM.

We are engaged in the vital spiritual enterprise of making the Truth known, that those who are seemingly in bondage may be set free. We must live consciously in the Reality of the Truth of ourselves. We must be more and more quickened in our understanding of the *Light* of life, so that we may be able to do more and more for the healing of others who walk in seeming darkness and lack of life. "I am come that they might have life, and that they might have it more abundantly," said Jesus.

As we walk in His Name and are conscious of the Spirit of life in Christ Jesus, we shall become perfect agencies of that Spirit which sets men free from the so-called "law of sin and death." We shall be agents of the Living Presence, of the Living God; agents of the Spiritual Gospel, of that pure and simple Truth which was in Christ Jesus.

He was the perfect Incarnation of God. He was the incarnate Word of the Father. Our goal is to be the pure incarnation of His Spirit. Our privilege is to be like Him — the incarnate Word, the incarnate Truth; and being such, we will also do good and heal all manner of sickness and disease.

# LESSON II

HE who does the best healing is he who sees nothing to be done. He sees nothing to be done because he is seeing God only. He is at one with the Consciousness of God in whose Mind there is no evil, no disease, no accident, no distortion.

"Behold Who hath created!" The wise and successful healer beholds Who hath created. He knows no other Creator and no other creation. He is at peace with the Truth.

When a case presents itself to him for relief and cure, he does not stir out of this peace. He does not accept the disturbance into his consciousness that he may deal with it. He turns wholly to the Father within himself. He accepts only God and deals only with the Truth of Being.

This is the way Jesus of Nazareth healed all manner of sickness and disease and deformity. In the world's eyes He did nothing; but with the inner eye He did all. It was a matter of consciousness on His part, and the healing was a reflection of that consciousness.

Nothing entered Jesus' consciousness but God, the Supreme and Perfect Being. He did not consider anything but the Father's Love for man, and His love for the Father. There was no division, no separation, in His mind. He did not look to the Father now and then. He walked with God, fully conscious of the Oneness of Father and Son and Holy Spirit.

17

If we would heal as Jesus did, we must awake in His likeness. We must be like Him; and to be like Him, we must know only God and His Son and His Glory. Jesus was livingly conscious of the Presence of the Father. He was God incarnate. He knew that God is All in all, and that beside Him there is none else.

In God there can be no sickness, pain, suffering, or any other pathological symptom. Jesus knew God, and that there is none else beside Him. He abode in that knowledge, and that was what did the work of healing. He did not study disease or its causes, and yet all manner of sickness and disease seemed to fade away in His presence. It was because of His singleness of eye; because of His knowing that God, the One Cause, was present, and that God is all the Presence there is. There is no other presence. If God be All in all, there can be no other presence.

Jesus knew the non-reality of so-called "matter" and its laws. He did not have to deny or affirm. He knew. If you do not know, it may be necessary for you to exercise your mental powers through denial and affirmation, but only if you do not *know*.

You may believe, but believing is not knowing. You may believe that there is a science of mathematics. You have seen mathematicians manipulate figures. Perhaps you have seen them in their rapid mental calculations, and you believe that there is a reason why they can do that. You have seen mathematics applied in various ways. You thoroughly believe that there is such a science, that there are people who have mastered this science, that there are master mathematicians; but that does not make you a master mathematician.

This is likewise true in regard to music. You may believe in the art of music. You may appreciate music, you may be enthralled by it. But that does not make a musician of you. This is the case in all arts and sciences, and so it is in spiritual science.

You may believe thoroughly in God, and in God as Spirit; but do you *know* it? Do you really know it? Do you know God? Can you say with the Apostle Paul, "I know whom I have believed"?

That is where we have to be as healers — we have to know. We have to be knowers, and we have to stand firm in that which we know, no matter what presents itself to us. No matter what the challenge may be, we have to meet it with our knowledge of the Truth.

Every so-called case that presents itself for healing is but a challenge to our consciousness. That is all it is. There is no reality in it. It is only an appearance, and we do not judge by appearances.

It may seem to be a very positive appearance. It may be very assertive. The one who presents himself may clamor for relief, and cry out because of his pain. He may seem to be suffering intensely, or he may have a soreness that to the eye seems very real.

In fact, most people like to present to you all the details of their condition, as you have undoubtedly observed. They like to show their wounds and their rashes and their eruptions and their deformities. They like to talk about their pains and describe them thoroughly to you and locate them exactly on their bodies. They are eager for you to give your attention to their troubles.

But if you are wise you will not do it, because that is not what you should be concerned with. You know that they have really come to you for relief, for healing, for freedom from these things that they try to describe to you. Your act of entering into their aches, or the description of their aches, will not heal them. You need to know the nothingness of the condition.

Sometimes, when you are healing, which is knowing the Truth, the case seems to get worse. It seems as though it were slipping away. You have a feeling that you are not adequate to the situation, that you are failing. Perhaps your patient cries out in disappointment and feels that you have not met the situation. He thinks that he has looked in vain for relief. Never mind what he thinks, for that point where the case seems to get worse is the point at which it is breaking.

If you will but remember and know that the Truth is nevertheless *all* the truth there is — that the Unsuffering, Unconditioned, Free Spirit is still All in all — you will be able to stand fast and not be at all concerned with the appearances.

But the neophyte very often becomes stampeded at this point, and is prone to retreat in the feeling that he or she has not sufficient wisdom and understanding to meet the demand. Keep your peace in God; for if your case has become worse during the treatment, it is a good sign that the word of Truth, which you have been speaking, has gone forth to do the work.

At such times, you do not need to speak the word again. You can abide in knowing only — knowing that the power of the Truth is now active. But you must abide wholly in the Spirit of Truth. If you will stand perfectly firm at this point, indifferent to the apparent situation and aware only of the Consciousness of God, you will have the joy of seeing your case come out of the seeming crisis and move toward health and freedom.

So I would counsel you who have not had much practice, if you should meet a case unlike any that you have met before and it seems to get worse under treatment, do not get into a crisis yourself. Do not concern yourself at all, except to see that in your own mind there is nothing but the knowledge of God, and that you are firm in that knowledge.

"Let there be a firmament in the midst of the waters."

It is at that point, that place, that very time when the surging waters of emotion or suffering or fear are seemingly overflowing the soul and apparently drowning it, that you must be a firmament, a firm mind. In the midst of the turbulent, seemingly blinding condition, stand firm with your eye single to one thing only — the Presence of God.

Do not be at all concerned with the symptoms or with the sounds. You are to hear only the Voice of the Spirit and not the voices of men. For always in a situation of that kind, the Spirit of Truth, which is the Spirit of Love, is definitely speaking; and if you will keep your heart attuned to the Spirit rather than to the flesh, you will be hearing and giving forth a potent word.

You may be given a message to transmit to the soul that seems to be in bondage, which shall be the one message, the only word, that could strike home to him. You will know it silently, and he will receive it. You will find that it is a freeing, healing word — the particular food which that soul was hungering for, the particular drink for which it thirsted. When you hear that word, you will pour it out; and you will realize that it is living water.

Every case is a challenge to the consciousness of the healer. It is for you to to ask yourself: "What do I know?" Not, "What does this person feel?" Not, "What are the people round about me thinking?" But, *What do I know?*"

That is always your question and your problem in a case of healing; and especially in times of crisis must you be firm in that which you know. You know the Truth, and the Truth shall make you free.

In your healing you are freeing your own consciousness of any misconception which you might be entertaining. You are freeing your own mind of ideas which you have harbored, perhaps for a long time.

If you will know that it is yourself that you are freeing you will realize that all consciousness is one consciousness, and all mind is one mind. You will detect the reason why the patient was presented to you, and you will be able to free not only the patient but yourself as well from some long-believed error or falsity.

In a certain sense, the cases that come to you are the reflections of your own consciousness. There is something in you that is in some way related to them. There is something in you that is akin to the situation. You might not be aware of it, because so many things that move in our consciousness are camouflaged, are disguised, so that we do not recognize their presence. But everything that happens to you outwardly is a reflection of some state of belief within your consciousness.

Therefore, all that comes to us as a problem is but a challenge, or call, for us to turn within our self and find "the Secret Place of the Most High," the Holy Place, the Healing Place, wherein we come face to face with God. For there is a point in consciousness at which one meets Divinity, and this is the Place that we must immediately find and enter.

According to the records as they stand, Jesus was not familiar with disease. In His healing, you will notice that Jesus never made overtures to a patient and never addressed Himself to a disease, but first turned to God, the Father, and then gave His word of command. *He did not concern Himself with the case.*

I keep emphasizing this because the natural way of man is to be upset by the symptoms that present themselves — the pain, the suffering, the groaning. If we are not careful, these things will touch a sympathetic chord in us, and sympathy never healed anybody in the world. So we must take heed that we do not enter into any sympathetic relation with the pathological case, because, if we do, we are quite likely to picture the condition in our own bodies. And then there will be two sick instead of one!

I have known people who had to withdraw from their healing practice, because they took upon themselves the symptoms of the cases that came to their attention. They gave their attention to the case instead of to God. Also, I have known practitioners who just got benumbed and unnerved by their sympathy. They mistook their sympathy for love.

A teacher once came to me about a child who was in a critical condition, apparently. Several physicians had been called in, and there had been a consultation in which they had decided that the disease was a tumor on the brain. The child was in a coma, and her heart was almost still. The teacher, who had been called in to treat metaphysically, described the child to me as "lying there like a piece of wax."

The physicians said that the only way to save the child's life was to operate. When the teacher heard them say that, she became stampeded. "My mother-nature rose up," she said to me, "and I was much distraught. Will you take the case?" You see, this teacher was not looking within to the Highmost. She was not watching the Truth. She was doing the opposite of what Jesus did, and taught us to do. So she lost her nerve, because she was watching the child; and nothing but fear out of her "mother-sympathy" was going forth to this child, instead of the word of Truth out of her consciousness of God.

Well, the child was restored to health, and it was not a tumor of the brain. You may meet something akin to this situation; so I will tell you how it was. The word of Truth brought to light the contributory cause of the trouble, and it was as I shall relate it.

This little girl had come running to her mother very jubilantly, all breathless and excited. It was a Saturday and school was out. Some of her playmates had said that they were going to have a party and had invited her to come; so she ran home to tell her mother that she was going. But her mother said, "You are not going." The child said, "I have to go. I said I would, I promised." But the mother said, "You can't go." Then the child said, "I *am* going!" The mother said, "You are not. I am your mother, and I say you're not going — and you aren't." The child asked, "Why not?" And the mother replied, "Never mind why. You can't go." The child kept on insisting that she must go until she had worked herself up into a tantrum. She threw herself on the floor and kicked and screamed. But the mother kept on saying, "No!" The mother's will was the stronger of course; so the child was mentally beaten into insensibility.

There wasn't anything wrong with the child's brain. Physically speaking, there was a violent contraction of the spinal muscles between the shoulders. All the muscles related to the upper spine were spasmed, and this had temporarily cut off, or interfered with, the circulation of blood to the brain. The child had been thrown into this state by the tension of wills clashing. There had been warfare on the mental battlefield; and the child, in her natural resistance to an unexplained hardness of will, became paralyzed with the tension of her mind.

Any such condition, however, can be immediately nullified by the word of Truth. Before the doctors could operate they were able to see that there was no tumor, and that no operation was necessary. When the healer abides in the Truth, knowing the nothingness of anything and everything that is unlike the Truth, his or her word of the Spirit dissolves the condition and restores the soul. The trouble was all mental. It was all falsity. As they say in the East, it was "just a dream of the senses, just *maya.*"

A healer must know the nothingness of a situation of this sort and not be concerned by the appearances, no matter how bad they may seem to be. Recall your attention again and again to that word of Jesus: "Judge not according to the appearance."

Never be fooled by any physical or material aspect that presents itself to you, for it is not true. It is the picture of an untruth, and an untruth is nothing. Nothingness has no substance, no intelligence, no objective, and no course. It is just nothing. Do you *know* that?

Always, in healing, you must know the absolute nothingness of the whole matter. Also, you must be able to stand firm in your knowing. You must be of a firm mind to know the untruth of a situation like that which I have just described.

Many healers are stampeded by an appearance of so-called cancer. It seems very real. People are frightened as they read the newspapers and are told, "Cancer is increasing; it is becoming one of the leading destructive agencies known to medicine." But the healer must not be like the people who do not know. By whatever appearance an untruth may present itself to us, it is but a challenge to our knowledge of the Truth, and that is the way we should meet it.

We should *know* the Allness of Truth and the nothingness of the appearance, and thus be able to stand firm against all appearances and announcements and descriptions of cancer or tuberculosis or meningitis or any other of the inventions which the imagination of man has formulated.

We must have the single eye that looks through and beyond the whole matter, that sees only the One Presence and Power and Glory, and knows that the Infinite Presence is All there is.

In the East, this singleness is spoken of as "the one-pointed mind." The healer must be one-pointed. His mind must be pointed toward One Thing — which is no thing. God has been called "The Great No Thing," because God is not a thing. God is Spirit. God is not subject to any conditions, diseases, or symptoms. God is not feeling any pain and cannot be made to feel any pain. God is not cognizant of pain or suffering. He does not behold or know what it is.

Neither must we behold or know what it is. We must see as God sees, and not be caught by appearances. We must walk in Reality and stand firm in that Reality. Then the appearance will change. The false belief which shows itself in the flesh will disappear into its native nothingness, for it is nothing, and the flesh will no longer be burdened by it.

As we learn of Truth and Wisdom and Love and Harmony and Order, there will be no discord or pain or suffering in belief, and therefore no physical picture of a false belief transmitted to the flesh. In Truth there is neither a false belief nor its outcome. So the healer who abides in the Truth does not look at the lie or the manifestation of the lie. Then it will not be there. To him whose eye is single it never was there and was not seen.

It is so important that you should give no attention whatever to appearances that again I repeat this counsel. You must not be governed or affected in any way by those things that present themselves to your outer eye. It is not by the seeing of the eye or the hearing of the ear that one should judge.

No matter how assertive the exterior condition may be, no matter how loudly the patient cries out to you and appeals to your sympathy, you must give him no thought. You must be firm in your inner knowing. You must judge *righteous* judgment.

Such an attitude on your part does not mean that you are unkind or unloving. On the contrary, it is evidence of the highest kindness and the strongest love. It may be a vital test, but you will know that your awareness of Love is dependable if you can stand firm and not allow one who is already in error to go deeper; if you can prevent one who is already in the bondage of false belief from being pricked harder and held more rigidly by it. It is an act of love to be able to stand and not give in to the appearance.

The people who do not understand what you are doing may say that your behavior is plain proof that you have no feeling. They may think that your attitude is not only unkind but inhuman. It is not inhuman, though we may say that it is "non-human," because it is divine.

Your office as healer is to lift people out of their inhuman, subhuman, undivine states of consciousness. It is to lift them up to the True Consciousness in which they too may stand firm, knowing their oneness with the Divine One and their freedom from all evil. You can do this the more readily if you will keep a conscious grip on your own mind by lifting up all your attention and all your love to the Perfect Truth.

So the fact is that, in treating your patient, you are

treating yourself. The healer is always the patient. That may sound strange at first, but you can see how it is so. You as the healer are healing yourself as the patient, and you as the patient are receiving the Truth of Being.

Therefore, it is for you to see that your own consciousness is clear, crystalline, pure, and not clogged by any falsity or error or untruth. Your heart and mind must not be oppressed by — or even aware of — any discord or inharmony; and you must be sure that you are not believing in any form or presentation of untruth.

You must have the single eye, open to the One Presence. You must let your thinking be charged with the dynamic force of the Spirit. The patient will catch this true positiveness; for there is always that Light of understanding within the patient which is at one with the Truth — that Light which is the very Truth Itself. It will respond and flame up and heal him, for it is the Divinity in us all. The I AM is in all, and it is the One I AM. When you touch It in your own consciousness, you touch it everywhere.

In treating, you are not treating a particular person. You are destroying some false belief that is being accepted as true. If you thoroughly destroy it, you will heal not only yourself and your patient, but you may heal thousands of others in various parts of the world. They will rise out of their sickbeds of pain, not knowing why they are well, but nevertheless well and free, because they were sensitive to the word of Truth that came to them. They will unknowingly respond to the state of consciousness with which you knowingly healed.

By "knowingly healed" I mean that you consciously knew

the Truth, and not that you did the healing; for it is always the Truth Itself that does what is called "a healing." So, when you are called upon to heal, your only problem is with yourself — that you may be filled to overflowing with the knowledge of God. If you will remember that and keep your eye single to the Allness of the Divine Being, you will come into that Presence and Power which shall go forth through you as a healing.

You will then be rewarded by the gratitude and acknowledgment of people who may write you from various countries of the world that they have received your word and knew that you were treating them. You were not treating them at all. You may not have known that they wanted your help, but they got well. They had simply looked toward you as an avenue of the Power of the Truth, and thus they received your state of consciousness. The True Consciousness in which you were abiding displaced the false one by which they had been misled, and they were restored to wholeness. Perhaps some of you have had that experience.

"Ye shall know the Truth, and the Truth shall make you free." And your conscious realization of the Truth will cause others to be set free; for whatever your state of consciousness may be, it will be communicated to others. They will catch it. Your so-called patients will reflect your consciousness, especially if they are very ill and in a very negative state. If they have reached out in faith, believing, and are looking to you perfectly, they will be open and responsive to your consciousness and your thoughts.

It is your duty, therefore, to keep your mind clear and free by abiding in the Truth. You must be in the Reality of the Truth constantly. If for any reason you seem to have lowered your consciousness, if in any way your vision has been deflected and you have dropped away from your awareness of the Truth, then you must withdraw at once into the Holy Place of your oneness with the Father.

Forsake everything and go alone by yourself, as Jesus did when He was hard pressed by the multitude. Then, when you have abode in the Silence until you have been lifted up to the Heights of Reality, you will come out with mind refreshed and heart serene, which will immediately benefit your patients. They will respond. They will become conscious of a restoration taking place within themselves. For we do not live to ourselves alone, nor in separation, nor in time and place.

God is timeless and spaceless. Man, as the son of God, is a spaceless being. God is omnipresent. Man, in the image and likeness of God, is also omnipresent. You are not geographically limited or bound. You are not circumscribed. Your consciousness travels, swifter than light, to the ends of the earth and beyond the earth into the immeasurableness of the heavens.

Remember, your consciousness is not an exclusive airtight piece of thinking. It is one with all consciousness, and all consciousness is one. We may say of consciousness what the Apostle John said of the Word: "In the beginning was the Consciousness, and the Consciousness was with God, and the Consciousness was God" — is God, for God is eternal. There is only one Consciousness — God.

God is All and in all. God is everywhere, at every point. He is present with equal Force and Power and Love and

Wisdom at every point. Wherever you are, you are in the center of the Kingdom of God. You are the very throne room of Deity. You cannot be where God is not. Where you *are* is centered all the Power and all the Wisdom and all the Love of God; and wherever that centering may be, it is likewise everywhere. God is He, or That — however you may wish to express it — whose center is everywhere and whose circumference is nowhere.

If you have studied physics, you may know that when force is exerted at but one point in frictional substance, it is found to be operating in every direction equally. The action is omnipresent in regard to the substance used for experiment. You may· have made this experiment with water in a jar. If so, when you exerted pressure at one point, you found that the same degree of force was equally operative at every point of the substance and was moving in every possible direction at one and the same instant.

That is the best illustration of the facts, and it may give you an idea of the Presence of God everywhere equally present — the whole Presence and Power, not just some of it. The entire Force, Intelligence, Wisdom, Power, and Love of God are at every point. This means all His attributes, all His gifts, all His Being. This is difficult for the human mind to comprehend, but it is true.

You know how it is with the radio. The broadcasting station sends out radio waves. These waves go in every direction. Receiving instruments may be set up at any point, in any position relative to the broadcasting station, for at every point the same waves may be received with the same force. If instruments of the same quality and sensitiveness were to be set up at every point in the world, they would all receive the same message simultaneously and with equal power.

This may give you a slight glimpse of the possibility of consciously hearkening to God wherever you are, of knowing that wherever you are, God *is* with all His Power. And again I remind you, not with some of Himself, but with *all* His Force and Intelligence and Wisdom and Mercy and Love.

If you can *know* that and realize the truth of it, if you can abide unwaveringly in that consciousness and that receptivity toward God's Whole Presence in the midst of anything that may challenge this truth, you will find that immediately God's Wisdom, Love, and Power will be active in you and for you.

But the Activity of God requires man, for God works by and through man. The Father works through the consciousness and capabilities of man, for man. It is always God that does the work in man. Man has only to know what is true.

Jesus knew that it is the Father who does the work. "I can of Mine own self do nothing," He said. "The words that I speak unto you I speak not of Myself: but the Father that dwelleth in Me, He doeth the works."

We must remember that and know that we do nothing. We do not do the work. Our task is to acquaint ourselves with Him who does do the work. "Acquaint now thyself with Him, and be at peace."

And if you are thoroughly at one with the Divine Peace, your patient will be at peace, no matter how intense had

been the pain he was suffering. If you are in the consciousness of Perfect Peace, your patient will come into that
Peace.

You have but one thing to dislodge, and that is your own
judgment. You have but one question to ask, and that is
"Where is my consciousness?"

"Be still, and know that I am God." Still your own mind.
Free it from all thought of agitation by abandoning yourself to the Presence of God. Healing will follow. You must
be able to be quiet in the Presence of the Divine One, who is
everywhere present. If you consciously touch Him where
you are, you touch Him everywhere. If you touch the
Oneness, you touch Omnipresence Itself.

That is the reason why you may heal at a distance, why
you may give the absent treatment which has been laughed
at by so many people. There is no absence and there is no
distance.

Those practitioners who can only do good work in the
presence of the patient are thinking in terms of time and
space. They are limited in their thought. If they would
lift their consciousness to the Omnipresence of the Spirit,
they would know that they are themselves everywhere at
once.

For we are not physical beings, limited, circumscribed,
living in a certain city in a certain state and county. We
are not citizens of one city, but of all cities, all states, all
nations. We are citizens of the whole universe.

When, knowing this, we live consciously in the whole
universe, realizing that it is a universe of love and of wisdom, of knowledge, power, harmony, health, purity, joy, and

satisfaction, then we shall be moving freely. We shall be walking in the Truth, and thus walking, we shall behold the Truth everywhere.

Those who had been with Jesus were changed so much that it was noticeable to others. They had been with Jesus; they were not the same as before. There was a subtle, though definite, transformation within them and about them. They had been walking with Him who was conscious of the Omnipresence of God, of His Love and His Goodness. Jesus' Consciousness was contagious, and they had caught the heavenly essence of it. The knowledge of the Presence of God is contagious.

We use the word *contagious* so much in reference to pathological conditions that it has been rather besmirched. But there is a Divine Contagion — the Contagion of Love, Wisdom, Strength, and Power. If we abide in the Truth, walk in the Truth, and are firm in the Truth, we are exercising the vital element which is contagious; and this will cause others to awake to the Truth — to awake, not by studying, but by the Divine Contagion of the Presence of God.

There are many people who are bookworms. I think that is a good name for them, for they are always gnawing and chewing at books. They chew right through book after book, but they are never fed and they are never satisfied. It is all to no purpose, for neither learning nor understanding comes by this sort of studying.

Those who spend their time just trying to learn are suffering from a form of lust. It is the lust for learning that urges them on, not the desire to live the Truth. So they never learn and they never know. "I am the Truth," says the Living Christ.

The knowledge of Truth comes through the heart by living it. You must let the Truth inhabit you to know it, and you must inhabit the Truth to understand it. Truth is Being. It is not a great quantity of information and ideas. Truth is Life. It is the Activity of the Eternal Light, the Christ, I AM, Omnipresence.

You cannot get *that* into your brain, but you can love it and live it with all your consciousness. To have your head crammed with a knowledge of facts, thoughts, methods, ways, and images, is just to know nothing at all.

"I am the Way, the Truth, and the Life." That is not what we call a fact. It is Life Itself. It is the Spirit of God. Living Knowledge comes from His Holy Spirit.

"Give me that knowledge that cometh not by learning," prayed Augustine, as he perceived the true way to know.

The Scriptures do not advise us to ask of man or of books for knowledge. They tell us to turn to the Source of knowledge from which all knowledge comes; to ask of God, who gives to every man abundantly of the Breath of knowledge.

To be still and confident in the Presence of God opens our minds to the Divine Wisdom, to the Soul Science, which is not of this world. In quietness and in confidence we are taught the great and mighty things of the Spirit, which the schools of philosophy and psychology know not. No man can impart spiritual knowledge to another by the intellect. Only through that other avenue, the intimate avenue of the Breath of the Holy Spirit, can any man truly receive and *know*.

Many of the people who are seeking Truth have formed such a habit of *seeking* that they are actually running away from it. There is no need to seek. The Truth is seeking you. Be still and know, and let the Father find you. "The true worshippers shall worship the Father in spirit and in truth: for the Father seeketh such to worship Him."

Do not seek to know, but be still and you shall know. If you abide in the Secret Place of the Most High, you cannot help knowing, and so you cannot help healing.

You see, the way of the Spirit is simple, not hard. "My yoke is easy, and my burden is light," says the Christ. The sense of feeling out after God is not the way of the Spirit. It is by the feeling of God as "closer . . . than breathing, and nearer than hands and feet" that we realize spiritual peace and spiritual power. Then, everywhere we are, everywhere we go, good work shall be done — not by us, but through our knowing of the Truth.

So shall we rest from our labors and our works will follow us, as was foretold in the Book of Revelation. We rest in the Oneness of God. We rest in the Omnipotence of God. We rest in the Omniscience of God. We rest from our own minds in God Himself.

If you choose, you can abide in the Secret Place with God. You can abide in power and light and strength and harmony and health and wholeness, in the Allness of the Spirit. So shall you receive knowledge with no struggle of seeking or learning. Knowledge will be given unto you.

Then you will have the joy of seeing others emerge from their darkness into light. They will behold the same great Light of the Truth that you are beholding; and they will

arise up out of the illusion of disease and suffering into
the joyous realization of peace and harmony, health and
wholeness.

## LESSON III

HEALING is the result of attainment and is secondary to the work within ourselves. Healing is the out-working, or out-picturing, of a certain state of consciousness into which the healer rises. If the healer is alive to the Truth, he inevitably touches that state of consciousness, that Oneness of God, which heals.

If we are wholly conscious of the truth that God is Spirit and that man is the offspring of God, a spiritual being — if we *know* this to be so, we shall find that healing will be done as quietly and easily as warmth is made manifest in a room when the radiator is charged with heat. The warmth of the room is inevitable, and likewise healing will be inevitable.

Healing will always be taking place through us if we walk in the consciousness of the Oneness and Allness of God, aware of only that One Presence and Power.

As we feel our union with the Divine and commune with Him who is within us, His Nature is revealed to us to a greater and greater degree. More and more shall we know the Spirit and the things of the Spirit. We shall be conscious of the Law of the Spirit and of the radiating Activity of the Spirit of Life. The attributes of God will no longer be mere words to us, but their essence, their very being, will be unfolded in our consciousness.

One of the chief attributes of God is Love. "God is Love," said John. "He that loveth not knoweth not God."

Love is a most potent power. It is the great healing

agency. Love for our fellow-man is essential to successful healing. John expressed this truth clearly, and we would do well to remember his words.

"He that loveth his brother abideth in the light, and there is none occasion of stumbling in him. But he that hateth his brother is in darkness, and walketh in darkness, and knoweth not whither he goeth, because that darkness hath blinded his eyes. . . . Beloved, let us love one another: for love is of God; and every one that loveth is born of God, and knoweth God. . . . If we love one another God dwelleth in us, and His love is perfected in us."

Love is life and it radiates life. If we wish for success in the realm of healing, we must have the feeling of love and kindness and good will toward our fellow-man. Our thought must be constantly directed Godward, for the Love we are speaking of is divine, not personal. Our hearts must be centered in the Spirit. "Incline your ear, and come unto Me," says the Spirit.

Love is the fulfilling of all law. If any man love God with his whole heart, he shall know what life is. He shall understand that the law of life is the law of love. So, to be successful healers, it is essential for us to cultivate the consciousness of good will and kindness and forbearance and forgiveness and tenderness and graciousness toward our fellow-man. For "he that loveth not his brother abideth in death. . . . If a man say, I love God, and hateth his brother, he is a liar."

Love is Life, Love is God, and God is the healing power. The Father within you — the Divine Love within you — does the work.

If ever you find yourself unsuccessful in a case of healing, look into your own heart. Do not treat people, but search your own heart. Do you love God with your whole heart, soul, mind, and strength? Is your whole being focused Godward? Are you concerned only with the Divine Spirit? Is your eye single? Or is there a grudge, a darkness in your eye? "If thine eye be single, thy whole body shall be full of light."

The practice of healing always resolves itself into self-treatment. We might say that healing is the practice of keeping our own consciousness clear and the direction of our attention fixed and established — firmly fixed on the One. "Thou wilt keep him in perfect peace, whose mind is *stayed* on Thee."

A healer cannot let his mind wander over many things. He cannot get distraught over conditions and circumstances and people. He should be feeling vital, alive, dynamic, charged with the Divine Energy and Power, and constantly aware of it.

If he is not, he must look into his own mind, for therein he will find the trouble that makes void his word for a patient. He will find that his mind is scattered, and so his forces are dissipated. If he is not loving God with all his being, he is not single-eyed.

To be a master of healing, one must love and live the Truth of God; one must abide under the Christ commandments. It is a life of consecration. It is a forgetting of self, a losing of self in the one great Life of Christ.

If any man would find his life, he must first lose it. "He that findeth his life shall lose it: and he that loseth his life

for My sake shall find it." Or, as John heard the Divine
Wisdom, "He that loveth his life shall lose it: and he that
hateth his life in this world shall keep it unto life eternal."

There are so many people who are seeking for life, trying to draw life unto themselves, searching and crying out
for more life. But Life is right at hand with all its power
and vitality, and it will show itself and work according to
its own law, wherever the channels and vehicles are open
and ready.

God is more willing to give than we are to receive. If
there seems to be a lack of life, it is because the channels
are not open. For the Divine Life is not absent but is ever
present; and being Love, it is radiant, or radioactive.

If you sometimes find that your word is impotent, and
your cases are not responding under your attention, it is
because your attention has been lowered. Perhaps your
attention is fixed on the case itself. You remember, in the
first lesson, we spoke of placing the attention elsewhere.
"Look unto Me, and be ye saved." Turn wholly to the
Divine. The Father does the work.

If you could only know that, really know that it·is the
Father that does the work, you would abandon yourself
completely to God. Then you would immediately become a
channel and avenue, through which and by which the Father
could work. You would be conscious of the Oneness of God,
and your so-called patient would catch some of that consciousness.

To the degree that the healer is aware of the Divine

Presence will the patient feel the healing. That Presence
will act as a fine, white fire — an essence moving through
the whole being, restoring and renewing and quickening and
healing. The Father does the work.

Again, if you have some particular case that is not responding, you may find that you have been critical somewhere toward something or somebody and thus dropped
your attention. When you have lowered your vision, for
the time being you do not feel the dynamic action of the
Spirit. You must lift your vision.

Perhaps there was something unlovely about the person
who presented herself, or himself, which you felt and saw.
Then you must look up and away, and behold the Divine,
and enter into the Presence of the Infinite Beauty. Your
eye will then be lighted with a new perception. You will
see deeper and further into the case. You will see through
it and beyond it to the Divine Presence.

Or perhaps your outer eye has caught the infirmity or
the pathological aspect of the case. But as you make nothing
of the appearance, you shall behold the glory of the Son of
the Supreme, and through your patient there will then shine
the Divine Power. There will be a quickening and a healing.

If you can keep yourself free from the sense of the physical aspect, and simply realize that the Presence of the Spirit
is the one and only Substance and Power, you will find, as
it were, a new birth taking place right before you. A person
might become a new creature then and there. It would be
quick. It would be just as soon as you had touched the
place of understanding and were aware of the Heavenly
Presence.

All our work, then, is to let ourselves be lifted up. "I, if I be lifted up from the earth, will draw all men unto Me."

Let us assume that you long to help people, but that no one comes to you for healing. This attitude of mind is not a pure channel for the works of the Holy Spirit. It is not loving the Truth for its own sake. It is not losing your life in Christ Jesus. Instead, it is seeing error which you think you can remedy.

That attitude does not help any one or draw any one. "I, *if I be lifted up,* will draw. . . . . " If you become aware of the Spiritual Nature of man and never lose sight of that truth; if you are concerned only with the elevating of your own mind, and your desire is only to be more conscious of the Spirit, you will not concern yourself with people, as to whether they come to you or not.

But, if you are radiant with the glory of the Divine, the people will come. If you are aware of your union with Him who is the Almighty, the Omnipotent, the one and only Power, the people will be drawn of the Father within you. They will hearken and they will hear.

"Thy people shall be willing in the day of thy power." Your power is the One Power. When you are conscious of your oneness with the One, the people will know it. They will come to partake of the water of Life that you are willing to give out so freely, without any thought of gain.

This applies also to those who are more gifted in teaching than in healing, and who would like to spread the Gospel of good tidings by teaching the Truth. So let us assume that you have found no students, or very few, to listen to you.

Well, in my many visits to classes and centers of teaching, I have found that where the whole thought was the love
of man and the love of God, and the pure desire to live in
fellowship and communion with the Spirit, there was always
a warmth and a glow and a fire and force at work — and
the people delighted to come there and learn. They were
drawn to the place wherein there was no thought of self
whatever, where life was lost in the One Great Life, and
where the mind was fully centered on the One, kept and
rested on God. In such places the law of the Spirit of life
was operative — powerfully so.

But where there was not that consecration and devotion
and abandonment of self; where there was, instead, a
reaching around and planning in various ways to attract,
to entertain, and to hold people, there was a coldness and
deadness, a lack of spiritual life. Where there is any fear
as to loss of prestige or power, where anyone is carrying on
his ministry as a business, there is not the glow and warmth
of the Spirit; and there is lacking that high, fine work which
could be carried on with perfect success by selflessness, consecration, and devotion.

So if the classroom is not filled, and the people do not
come to listen, it is because the message going forth is not
vital. It is because the teacher and his place of teaching are
not charged with the dynamic Power and Love of God. Do
not blame the people for not coming. Do not think that they
are stupid not to listen to all you have to say about God.
They do not want your philosophy. They are thirsting after
the water of life. They want to feel the contagion of the
Presence of God. They are hungry for Reality, for the Love

that is God. God is Love, and if you have chosen to be a messenger of Love, there must not be any fear, jealousy, competition, or worldly effort in your consciousness.

Therefore, abide in the Secret Place and commune with the Eternal Spirit. Whether you are a teacher or a healer or both, you are an avenue for God's business, not your own; for God's Presence, not your own. When you know that, the multitude will hasten to you to be fed.

It is only he who loves, abandoning himself and losing his life for the sake of the One Life, who can become a channel through which that Life can work. The eye must be single; the mind must be stayed on the ONE. Into the mind that is stayed on God there enters the great peace, and peace is one of the essential medicines of the divine pharmacopoeia. The healer must be possessed of peace in order to do potent, lasting work.

The healer must be aware of that Spirit of peace that "passeth all understanding," for the Divine Peace is something that the human mind does not understand. It is something that cannot be described. You can know whether or not you have it, but you cannot tell what it is because the things of the Spirit are beyond description. They are divine; they are infinite. You know them by an inner knowing.

If your mind is lifted and stayed on the Divine, there will come and rest in you this very peace which passes understanding. It is always the first, and may be the only medicine needed in a case — just that the Divine Peace may be felt. It is powerful when it is in action.

Peace is one of the most dynamic manifestations of the Spirit that there is. It is not inaction; it is intense action, so intense that the mind cannot register it. Perhaps you have looked at something which was moving so fast that your eye could not register any motion and the object seemed to be perfectly still. That is the way with the Divine Peace. It works with such a high potency that the mind cannot comprehend it. So dynamic is it that where it is felt it will change the whole structure of a man's consciousness in the twinkling of an eye. We need to have that peace to be successful healers. And we shall receive it by looking to the Divine and by keeping our eye on Him constantly.

It is possible to do that. It takes training because the human mind is prone to wander. Your mind interests itself in so many things that it is difficult to fix and to hold it to the One until you are aware that there is no other presence, power, substance, or intelligence than the One. But this single-minded awareness is necessary, and the way to attain it is to keep practicing until it becomes involuntary.

You have to call your mind back from its wanderings and place it again and again in the Divine Presence, which, you will remember, is always right where you are. After a while, if you will practice faithfully, the time will come when you will walk freely and constantly in the Divine Consciousness. It will never forsake you.

"Turn unto Me, and I will turn unto you" is the law of the Spirit. If you have turned and turned and kept recalling your mind again and again from its wanderings, you will gradually become fixed and established in the Spiritual Consciousness; and when that is done, there will be a continual healing potency at work through you. God works in and through your consciousness of Life. When you truly realize that Life is everywhere and that there is no place or point in space where Life is not, you will know that Life is everywhere *in all its fullness*, and that it is always working. You will know that the Life Principle is ever active.

Peter was so aware of the Divine Life that when the sick were brought near to him, they were healed by his shadow. If we would have that Life-consciousness as Peter had it, we must turn and give ourselves always, as he did, to the One.

We enter into that Consciousness by the abandoning of self, by the giving up of self entirely, by the taking of that attitude which St. Augustine expressed when he prayed: "I ask nothing of Thee. I do not ask even Thy love. I want only Thee." Willing to give all for the One and the knowing of the One, he was lifted up and transformed, his mind made radiant and alive and scintillating with intelligence and power. When we ask nothing for ourselves, not even the power to heal, we are also lifted up and the power goes forth through us.

Many people have said to me, "How can I get the healing power? I wish I had that power. It must be wonderful. I would like to get it." Well, as you know, all truth is paradoxical. So the way to get it is not to want it, but to want to know God. "I ask nothing of Thee. I do not want even Thy love. I want only Thee."

"Thine is the Kingdom, and Thine is the Power, and Thine is the Glory." When we can say that understandingly and truly abandon ourselves to that Truth, as the great ones have done, we shall see that we can have nothing of ourselves, for God is All.

"The earth is the Lord's, and the fulness thereof; the world, and they that dwell therein." All is the Lord's. When, therefore, we can become empty of self, when we want nothing and ask for nothing and reach up for nothing, but abandon ourselves completely to the Oneness of the Divine, we find Life.

Paul was an educated, cultured, erudite man. He was a scholar and a man of affairs and importance, headed for social and religious prominence. But he was willing to unlearn all that he had learned. He was willing to be accounted a fool for Christ's sake. He was willing to let go of all that he had, all that he knew, all that he cared for, all that he was, for the One; and he found that One.

So it is with our ministry. By our surrender of ourselves, by our indifference as to having the healing power, we find that power. For in so far as we realize that we are nothing of ourselves, we know that God is All, and that man is one with that All.

If we can follow after Christ and let go of self, not wanting to do anything, not wanting to be great healers and teachers, but looking only unto Him, we shall find that we have become fit vehicles through which the Divine will work.

Then, like Peter, we may cast a shadow of healing. The word going forth from us shall accomplish that whereunto it is sent. We shall declare a thing and it shall be established unto us. The power that shall go forth will be the Power of the Spirit. There will be a quickening energy, a subtle dynamic, in our word which shall do the work. It will not be in what we *say*, as so many people think, but in what we *know* and what we *are*.

You remember the words of Emerson which are so often quoted: "Do not say things. What you are stands over you the while, and thunders so that I cannot hear what you say to the contrary." That is true, always true, in spiritual things. And what you think in your heart, what you know in your soul, what you dwell upon in your belief, determines what you are. What you *are* is what goes forth from you.

So if you are charged with the dynamic of the Spirit, if you are aware of the Oneness of God and awakened to His Life within you, you can say to a man, "The moon is made of green cheese. Don't you know it?" And he will get up and be well. It is not what you say; it is the Spirit within that does the work. It is that which goes out from under your tongue that counts, no matter what goes out over it. There is a silent word going out from under the tongue, and this is heard independently of that which goes out over the tongue. It is this silent word which the patient hears and to which he responds.

Therefore we should not be so much concerned with our word as with our consciousness. We should see to it that our consciousness is clear, that we are abiding in the Oneness of the Divine, that we know the Truth. We must be sure that the Truth is not just theory or belief or hope with us, but that it is Something we know, and *know* that we know. This is said to be wisdom. "He who knows, and knows that he knows, is wise."

The healing power is active in him who knows and *knows*

that he knows, for thus he is alive throughout his whole being to the Presence of the Spirit, which works in and through him to will and to do. "Wisdom giveth life to them that have it," said Solomon. "Wisdom is the principal thing; therefore get wisdom: and with all thy getting get understanding. . . . A wise man is strong; yea, a man of knowledge increaseth strength."

Wisdom and understanding and love are members one of another, and we "get" them by not allowing ourselves to stand in the way. We need to get our minds out of the way — these minds that are so concerned and worried about circumstances and conditions, so anxious about things and appearances, so upset by what others do or say or think. All such mental activity must get out of the way, so that the Activity of the Mind of God may be All in all through us.

We do not need to concern ourselves with people, but we do need to concern ourselves with our own consciousness — to keep it free and open to the Spirit. And we can keep open to the Spirit only when we have no fear of loss or failure.

But if we are concerned about our financial welfare, we are putting up thoughts and feelings which are in the way of the free action of the Free Spirit. The having to plot and plan and scheme and work for financial welfare is not righteousness. Instead, "seek ye first the Kingdom of God, and His Righteousness; and all these things shall be added unto you." In His Kingdom and His Righteousness your welfare already exists. It manifests itself for you, without any effort on your part, when your consciousness rests in God's Consciousness.

Let us leave behind us all our search for human knowledge, all our desire for learning. Let us turn often to that singleness of mind in which Augustine prayed, "Give me that knowledge that cometh not by learning." For it is not by the mechanism of the intellect that we can know and understand. Knowledge and understanding come into the mind with the sweet stream of inspiration from the Heights of Wisdom, from Omniscience Itself — which is closer to us than our own breathing.

"The Comforter, which is the Holy Ghost, whom the Father will send in My name, He shall teach you all things." The Holy Spirit will teach us right here where we are. It will teach us what no man can teach us. It will uncover the mysteries of the heavens to him whose eye is single, whose mind is one-pointed. But we cannot hear the teaching of the Spirit when we turn away from the Divine to human ways and human learning. As Paul said, it is but "foolishness with God" to get so wise with the letter of the law that we fail to receive from Him who alone can give us to know by the Breath of Truth.

"What things soever the law saith, it saith to them who are under the law." So if we are listening to the law, we are in bondage to the law, and our ministry will be of the letter of human learning. This is "the ministration of death," says Paul. "For the letter killeth, but the spirit giveth life." Only by the Spiritual Word are we born again into the grace and freedom and understanding of Life.

How many of us hearken to the Spirit? How many of us know that we are now redeemed from attention to the law by the Spirit of Christ, in whom is our real life? Our real life is our awareness of the Divine, which is Spirit. Our healing ministry is to know the Spirit and be quickened by the Spirit.

If you will hearken to the Spirit, walk in the Spirit, commune with the Spirit; if you will be still and know the Spirit, and in quietness and confidence wait upon the Divine, you will feel that Force which is the Vitality and Energy of the Spirit. Your mind also will receive instruction in all things. You will hear the Voice of the Spirit, and there will be formed in your consciousness new concepts, new realizations. You will be taught from on High.

"I will instruct thee and teach thee."

"I will answer thee, and show thee great and mighty things, which thou knowest not."

"I will lead them in paths that they have not known."

The abandoning of one's self, the letting go of the mind, the opening of the heart to the One Presence and Power, causes the heart to glow and shine, and the mind to be vibrant with understanding. The winds of wisdom and plenty will blow toward him who gives himself up to the One. The idiosyncrasies and obsessions that formerly accompanied him will dissolve and move out into nothingness, and in their place he will hear the heavenly Word.

Likewise in healing, if you will be still and know and hearken, you will receive the perfect word for your patient. God is ever speaking to the soul, but we do not always listen and hear. Be not dull of hearing with your spiritual ear. Listen in stillness for the Voice of the Spirit.

Hearing the word of Truth, you shall speak it — but not to your patient. Just speak it. When you have hearkened, your patient will hearken, and he will understand and know.

He will walk out of his illness, and the glory of Sonship will shine in and through him. It will be your satisfaction to see an apparent change in him, but you will know that there was no change, that the glory of the Son of God was always within him. He has not really changed at all.

You have not created Truth by speaking the word of Truth. The Truth always was and always will be. You do not cause the Truth to be Truth. But those who look on and judge by appearances are seeing that a change has taken place, and they will call it a healing. You will know that there was nothing to be healed. God did not need healing, and God was all there was. A lie does not need any healing. You cannot heal a lie, because a lie is nothing. So there was not any healing.

The moment you find out that a lie is a lie, you see that it has no power, no intelligence, no purpose. You know that it is nothing. But it was nothing all the time, whether you knew it or not. It was only when you believed the lie to be true that you became involved with it. When you are thoroughly acquainted with the Truth you will be free of lies, and you will never be disturbed by anything that is contrary to the Truth. You will know that "I am the Lord; I change not." From everlasting to everlasting the Truth is always the same.

When you healed your patient, there was not any healing done. And yet there was; but it was all in appearances, for there was no reality in the sickness. Then if there was no reality in the sickness, there was no reality in the healing. And if you did not heal anything, you are not a healer, are you? People may say you are. Let them say so; but you may keep on knowing that you are a knower of the Truth.

It was the same with Jesus. He went about healing all manner of sickness and disease, but He did not do anything. He just walked in the realization of that Truth to which nothing can be added and from which nothing can be taken. The Truth simply *is* in all its glory and power. Jesus knew the Truth and spoke it, but He did not create it. You cannot create it either, but you can *know* it.

When you know the Truth, there will be a freeing from untruth. The freeing will come forth because you have waked out of sleep, because you know that God is always All in all and that there is never any other presence or power or substance or intelligence. When you see that, you will not try to heal. Practitioners who make a great labor of healing by working on their patients do not get along very fast, because they are trying to do something that does not need to be done.

God is all there is, and you cannot change Him. You cannot do anything with Him or to Him or for Him. You can only walk in His Presence, and be awake and alive to that Presence. But when you know God's Presence, there will be that something in you, with you, and about you, which is called "mastership." We can compare it to the musician who is thoroughly trained in music, thoroughly imbued with the science and the art of it, and so has "arrived," as we say, and is a master.

Now the genuine musician detects any discord at once. He knows when there is any violation of the principle of music because he is so completely grounded in the nature of music that he immediately senses an incongruity. But this does not distract or change his knowledge and understanding of music itself. He does not believe that the errors and ignorance of some composition or performance are true music just because he hears them. His mind has been trained and saturated with the true science and order of music. His soul is full of the truth and essence of music. He does not just believe; he knows. No matter how small or how great may be the falsity that he hears, it does not affect his musicianship in the least. His mastership is not influenced or moved.

What is more, let us suppose that there is only one singer in a whole choir who has the proper note and key, and that all the rest are off key. If that one will keep to the true key and tempo, ignoring all the rest and singing correctly, they will all swing into the right way and soon be together with that one. This will happen, not because the true singer has given any attention to their lack of musical accuracy, but because he has kept his own accuracy, because he has maintained his knowledge and his expression of the principle of music.

Thus it is in spiritual science. If you can keep to the Divine Principle yourself, you will find that the seeming discords of others will pass away.

And that is the way it is in healing. You become hypersensitive. You sense the slightest false thought that comes to that sensitiveness. You sense it, but you give no attention to it. You keep on with the Principle of Truth. You know the Truth and you hold to the Truth. You make the Truth more and more real to your consciousness. You do not let the inharmony and discord get you, and you do not

care about them. You care about the Truth. You keep true
to the Spirit of peace and joy, to the Goodness of God, to the
Holiness of the Spirit. As you abide in that peace and love,
the discordant note will cease sounding. The discord and
falsity will fade away into nothingness.

"Ye shall know the Truth, and the Truth shall make you
free." And if you are free, the patient also will become
aware of the Divine Freedom.

Do you see how it is? If you are all worked up in your
effort to help a person, your eye is on something that is
not God, because God would not stir you up like that. God
gives you peace and joy. If you are struggling and straining in your mind concerning some condition, you are giving
a false reality to that condition. You are magnifying a lie
and fastening it onto the consciousness of the afflicted person. By so doing you are simply using a form of hypnosis.
You may not realize it; but, for a negative subject, you are
making the condition appear even more real to his consciousness than it was before you tried to treat him.

It is unwise to struggle and strain in healing. If you are
doing that, you are recognizing the non-Godlike, and your
eye is not single. You are giving expression to falsity. So
long as you do that, the Spirit of Truth will not work in
your mind and through your consciousness.

Always remember that we ourselves are our patient, and
that it is not the other fellow, though we think and speak
of him that way. Nevertheless, we are the patient; we are
the one that must arise; and we must remember that, even
if we speak of someone else as our patient for the sake of
convenience.

It is for us to keep our own consciousness clear and free and uplifted. We must not be stampeded by any appearance that presents itself, nor feel that it is our duty to heal some case. It is our duty to be true to the Truth, to know the Truth, and to abide in the Truth. If we do this, the Free Power that is the Dynamic of the Spirit will work through us and alter the whole situation.

When we keep watching God, instead of man, we will not be at all concerned by any form of illness that has expressed itself physically. We will not be interested in its pathological aspects. We will simply concern ourselves more and more with the Truth. We will know that the picture in the flesh is merely a shadow cast by a false state of consciousness, a false belief of some sort.

The situation is not physical nor material, no matter what it is — even if it is a broken bone. It is entirely a state of consciousness or a shadow cast by some false idea. We are concerned only with consciousness, only with the mind. We do not judge by the flesh.

Jesus judged no man after the flesh. So, no matter what aspect is evident in man's flesh, we will not judge him by that. We will know the non-reality of the condition. We will pay no attention to the appearance. We will judge righteous judgment. The Jesus Christ judgment is true and righteous altogether, for Christ could see the true nature of man through all the shadows that were played before him, and He knew that all men are children of the Most High.

Therefore, having seen that it is man's mind and not his flesh which has occasioned the disturbed appearance, we must look through the mists and miasmas of the mind to see Reality. We must keep always beholding the glorious Presence of the Divine everywhere. That is what Jesus did, and what we need to do. "Follow Me," He said.

We must have that Mind that was in Christ Jesus. If we have it, we shall be hypersensitive. We shall be aware of falsity, but we shall not be moved by it. We shall not be carried away or hurt by it. Steadily beholding the real being of man, we shall say to the unreal, "Get thee behind me, Satan"; and then we shall only the more see the Truth. So shall we simply walk in the straight and narrow way of the Spirit; while the Spirit dissolves the appearances.

It is a narrow way that we must walk. "Few there be that find it," said Jesus. The men of the East say that it is so narrow you can hardly see it. But if our eye is single, we shall see it. If our eye is single to the One Presence and Power, we shall find ourselves moving along that line of integrity, and we shall see the falsity of sickness and disease fade away as we go forward in the Truth.

As we proceed in consciousness along the path of Truth, we shall continue to see errors and their results in flesh and circumstance, but there will be this great difference: We shall be untouched by them. We shall pass through them by the light of our knowing that they are not true. So we shall be in the world but not of it.

By the Light we shall be prospered, and by our steadfastness to the Light we shall lift others out of their fear of lack and deprivation and loss. We shall know that there is no such thing as famine; for we shall be living on the

Bread of Life, partaking of the Divine Substance, and awakening others to the abundance that is provided for the children of God.

We are children of Light and not of darkness. We are born of the Day and not of the night. We are born to walk in the Light of Love and Peace and Joy. Joy is always lightsome. Peace is always lightsome, and it tends to lift us above the earth and its so-called law of gravity. It lifts us and levitates us into a higher atmosphere, and we rise, free of our burdens, because of the great strength that is ours from the Spirit.

"I will put My Spirit in them." That Spirit is the Spirit of power and might and strength and wisdom and understanding. If we walk in that Spirit, we shall cause others to behold the Light. When they look up, it will be easier for them to see it because we see it. And when they see it, they also will know their true nature as children of Light. By the Light they will depart from their heavy-heartedness. They will begin to walk lightly and strongly as the strong sons of God which they are.

## LESSON IV

THE Scriptures say that God is "all, and in all," and
that "God is Love." God is omnipresent, God is omnipotent, and God is Love. God knows Himself; and since God
is Love, God knows Himself as Love. God knows himself in
man as Love, and He gives expression to this Self-Knowledge in man's being, of which the outer form or symbol is
the heart — the central organ of man's body.

We always use that word *heart* as referring to the center,
the fundamental, or root. If we are dealing with a subject
and we are getting the essence of it, the foundation of it, we
speak of getting to the heart of it. We can then understand
it, for the heart of a subject extends throughout its entire
constitution and is, indeed, the life of that subject.

It is the same with man. The heart is the center of his
constitution, and the blood is that fluid that moves through
the heart and out from the heart to his whole organism,
extending its life throughout the body. And so the Scriptures speak of the blood as the life of the body. The heart
is the seat of love. But love and life and light are one. So
the blood, being life, is also light as well as love. The Divine
Manifestation of God is Life, and that Life is the light of
man.

Few people know that the blood is luminous. And the
more a man is conscious of his Source, and his relation to
the Giver of all life, the more luminous in him is the blood.
The more he is aware of his Sonship, which means his radio-
activity or his expression of the Divine, the more will the

element of light be found in his blood.  God is Life, and Life is Light.

"In Him was life; and the life was the light of men." was John's witness of the Christ-Man.  As the Son of God, Man is the radiant expression of God.  The Son expresses the Life of the Father.  He is the manifestation of God's Consciousness of Himself as Love, as Life, as Light.

When there is a disturbance in the mind of man which has in some way disrupted his soul's relationship with the Divine as the Source of love and life, there is often a disturbance in the blood stream and in the organ called the heart.  In treating we are not concerned with the organ as such.  We remember that man is a spiritual being.  We know that he is the manifestation of God who is Spirit.  So we are interested in man as a spiritual being and not in his physical or outer expression.  We turn to the invisible, to the divine, to the inner nature of man.

All man's diseases are of the soul, or psyche.  The soul is disturbed when it is not reflecting the Divine Consciousness.  In its sense of lack or absence of the Divine, the mind takes on untoward conditions.  It is these mental conditions that we deal with by knowing their non-reality, by giving our attention to the Eternal Over-Soul, the pure Consciousness of God.

The healer looks to the *Source* of life and light.  He is of course aware of the fact that there is an outer organ called the heart, but he does not deal with that.  He gives his attention to the truth that God manifests Himself in man, and that man is the image and likeness of God, the expression of God.  A so-called heart trouble can usually be traced back to the fact that the man's, or woman's, love is not inclined toward the Divine.

"Incline your heart to the Lord God."

"Thou shalt love the Lord thy God with all thy heart."

"Acquaint now thyself with Him, and be at peace."

People are so concerned with the external side of life, so busy with form and symbol, and so-called material things, that they forget their Divine Source and are not aware of any conscious contact with God. They are not aware of being *really* the sons of God, expressions of the Most High One, divine manifestations.

When the Greeks of old said, "Know thyself!" that is what they meant. They did not mean that man should study the outer picture of "form and confusion," but that by knowing his relation to his Source and by acquainting himself with that Source, man would come to know his own nature. We have believed that the study of mankind reveals man to himself. But "Acquaint now thyself with Me, and know I AM" is the counsel of the seers of the Spirit. Remember That from which you came. If we are to know the Self, we must ever turn our attention to the Source, the Most High One.

When we acquaint ourselves with the Divine, we discover that the Nature of God is Love, and we see that Love is the creative Principle of Life. Then, as we realize what the Divine Love *is,* we shall see ourselves in our real relation to God. We shall find that we are related to the Divine in a mysterious way, a mystical way, and that when we maintain our knowing of this relationship, it will express itself outwardly.

If we are aware of God as Love and know our relation to that Love as sons of it, we shall be filled with a great strength and life and light. Our hearts will be *whole*. Our hearts will be free and unburdened. They will extend into Eternity.

In man's body, the organ of the heart extends itself throughout his entire organism by means of the arterial and venous systems. The physical heart is not located solely at one point in the breast, but extends itself to the very outermost of our bodies. We cannot prick the skin with the smallest instrument without piercing the heart; that is, without cutting a capillary and causing the life blood to flow. The heart is everywhere through the life fluid, and the life fluid is everywhere present throughout the entire body, including even the marrow of the bones.

There is an ever active cooperation between the heart and the bones. People think that bones are a hard, impenetrable part of their anatomy, but this is not so. They are soft and pliable and porous. They are penetrated by the capillaries of the blood, which carry forth the blood corpuscles from their inmost center. There is a great chemical process constantly going on within the bones, for the blood corpuscles are formed within them.

The bones are the foundation of the structural economy of man's body, just as the heart is the foundation of its organic economy. People generally speak with entire confidence when they say that they know something "because I feel it in my bones." There is a reason back of this saying; for the bony structure, in its vital co-partnership with the heart and the life blood, symbolizes the foundation of man, and that foundation is the Divine Consciousness. It is the beauty and symmetry of the Conscious Mind of God which thinks and works and accomplishes by means of man as an avenue or agent of its expression.

So the Divine Life manifests itself at the heart of our being, and we speak of the heart as the instrument of love. The words *heart* and *love* are used almost interchangeably, and are thought of as meaning the same thing. God is Love and manifests Himself as Love. "He that loveth not, knoweth not God; for God is Love."

Love is always radioactive, always giving of itself, always pouring itself out. And so we have the organ of the heart reflecting this truth in our bodies. For the heart pours itself out, as it were, and extends itself through all the tissue of the body, and then — through its extensions — pours forth the life blood, the living force, which carries nourishment and strength to every part. "Keep thy heart with all diligence; for out of it are the issues of life."

The blood carries light and air. You are probably more or less familiar with anatomy and physiology. You know that the blood is sent from the heart to the lungs where it is oxygenized and purified. The oxygen comes out of the illimitable ethers all roundabout, charged with sunshine; and it is because the blood receives and is infused with this vitalizing oxygen that all the worn-out and useless products of the body are taken care of and the tissues renewed. Also, it is the contact of the oxygen with the blood which moves the blood throughout the arterial system.

The root meaning of the word *artery* is "a carrier of air." The arteries are air-carriers. They carry the finer essences out of the ethers to the various parts of the body. And thus in every cell of man's organism an oxygenizing takes place which produces a combustion and a freeing. That is the force that carries the life-substance through the body. It is not pumped through. It is carried by the blood through the arteries by a finer energy than electro-magnetism. That energy has a resemblance to electro-magnetism, but is much finer and higher than any force the engineer knows. It is transcendent, and cannot be caught or held. It is the Breath of the Almighty.

Every time we breathe we are really breathing the Divine Breath. Elihu understood that when he said to Job, "The Spirit of God hath made me, and the Breath of the Almighty hath given me life." The seers of the East speak of the whole physical universe as being the outbreathing of Brahma, or God. Breath is Spirit, and Spirit is Life; and that Life is imparted to the blood when it contacts the lungs. The life breath goes through the whole organism and returns again.

The food that we eat, after being duly acted upon by mastication, saliva, gastric juice, and so forth, becomes a substance which the blood can pick up. The blood acts upon it and then carries it to the various parts of the body, distributing the elements of the food to the right places at the right time. Each little cell of the body is waiting for its own specific food, and receives that which nourishes it and builds it into the structure that enables it to play its part in the whole physical economy. It is evident that a great intelligence and harmony and order is working all through the body.

If we trace the food that we eat back to its ultimate source, we shall see that we are eating the Divine Substance. Our food in general consists of vegetables, fruits, grains, fish, and meat. Those who eat meat are eating that which has already partaken of the vegetables, fruits, and grains. These vegetables and fruits take their substance out of the air, and out of the earth in the form of water (which is oxygen and hydrogen), making carbohydrates, and so forth.

Since the sunshine that impregnates the earth and the water is also taken in, we find that our vegetables and fruits are simply the planet formulated in such a way that we can use it for nourishment. The plants live on the sunshine. The water is impregnated with and vitalized by the sunshine; the earth is impregnated with and vitalized by the sunshine; and the sunshine comes from the sun. Back of the sun is the Divine, the Spiritual Son. Back of all is God.

In that sense, when we breathe, we breathe God; and when we eat, we eat God. God is all life. If the sunshine, the air, and the food substance were to be taken away, in a short time there would be no life in the body. So God is our bodily life, as well as our spiritual life.

There is but One Source and One Life — God. We depend upon Him. Our life is provided by God. Our strength is provided by God. We are the products of the Divine Providence. We live and move and have our being in Him, and He works in us both to will and to do.

If we can see the truth of this, if we can realize it and know it, there will be a great sense of gratitude welling up in our hearts. Whenever there is gratitude in the heart, there is always a quickening and strengthening of the heart action. There are certain forms of heart trouble that are simply due to a lack of gratitude in the heart. If one can be awakened to a realization of his entire dependence upon the One Source, if he can know *who* he is and *what* he is and feel a conscious union with the Divine, that particular form of heart trouble will disappear.

Sometimes there is a disturbance in the heart because we lack the right feeling of affection and love. We have forgotten to love God "because He first loved us." We have forgotten that God *is* Love, and that Love outpours Itself. God constantly gives all that He is and all that He has to the object of His love, His offspring.

If we forget our sonship, if we do not acknowledge that sonship and pass it on toward our fellow-man in the form of good will, kindness, tolerance, forgiveness, and love, there may be a disturbance in the heart action. And so we are impelled to return to our remembrance of the Father and the Son, in whose Love we may find our Source and our true nature and being.

The healer is ever doing that. We might say that healing is that perfect realization of Love which calls man to remembrance, which brings him back to his sonship. Man has forgotten his sonship, and seems ignorant of his vital relationship with the Divine. He acts as though he were not in union with the Father of life, the God which *is* Life and forever gives life. That Life is the light of man, the light of his mind, the light that gives him intelligence — the power to perceive and to know.

The power of perception expresses itself outwardly through the eyes. The well-grounded and well-trained physician can often read from the eyes that there is a disturbance in the heart. He will know that in certain forms of eye trouble there is nothing troubling the eye itself. But the metaphysician will go further than the physician and find that there is a lack of appreciation in the consciousness, a lack of understanding on the part of the individual. He seems to be walking in his sleep. He is not awake. He is not aware of what he is, and does not recognize his relation to his Source.

The conditions that we find in the physical body are not physical. The body is not physical, though we use that term for it. Man is a spiritual being entirely. His nature is spiritual. The Source from which he came is spiritual — Divine Spirit Itself. Man is not a material being, and sickness is not a material manifestation. Sickness is evidence of mental disturbance, of double-mindedness and wrong beliefs which occasion discord and disharmony in man's consciousness.

So the healer who is wise, who thinks spiritually, can ignore the outer manifestation, except as he may understand the correspondence between the mental condition and the outer appearance. He may read backward from the symbol, or shadow cast, to that which has cast the shadow, but he is not interested in the shadow. And though he may read back into the nature of the shadow, into the false consciousness of the patient, yet his principal concern is with the true consciousness of the inner man. That is, he absorbs himself in the Divine Remedy — the Truth of God and man, which is not two but One Truth.

In nearly all forms of illness, there is trouble somewhere along the avenues of circulation. The circulation is impeded or disturbed. This is due to the fact that man does not know that God is Love. We are more apt in knowing God as Power. We can conceive of Him as the Almighty, the great Power that moves through the universe as Law, or the creative Energy that caused the universe to be, and which drives it onward. But we are not aware of God as Love.

It is essential for us to know God as Love and for us to know, also, that we are the loving offspring and the beloved offspring of the Supreme. It is simple and satisfying for us to love God, for "we love Him, because He first loved us."

If we become conscious of the Divine Being as Love, we begin to see Love as Life and Light. We will then see that Love is reflected outwardly — in man's body — as the purification of the blood stream, and as the harmonizing and regulating of the heart. We will see how dependent we are upon that Love, and how every manifestation in the outer world is an expression of the Divine Love.

It is the outpouring of the Spirit of Love behind the sun toward which the sun-worshippers looked. They did not worship the sun. They were reaching up for that which is behind the sun, for that which is the Cause of the sun's being. They felt the mysterious Power and Intelligence that had made the sun and caused it to shine with the light and warmth which could be drawn in by the earth-planet. They recognized that there was a Source which gave life and energy to all things on the earth, including themselves.

When we can see that there *is* that Power behind the sun which is the Cause of the sun, and that the sun in turn is the cause of life in the vegetable kingdom, and that the vegetable kingdom in turn gives life to man's body through the food that he eats, we then see that God — shining through vegetables, fruit, grains, and animals — is shining through man. The shining of the sun is the outpouring of the Infinite Love.

We live by the Love of God and upon the Love of God. The Divine Love gives life and light and nourishment to us. Everything we eat comes from God. It does not originate in the earth; it comes from God. When man is not aware of the One Source, when he does not believe and does not acknowledge it, he places his source of life and support and supply in the earth. He thinks that his sustenance is of the earth. That is the reason why his mind and his affairs get into such a state of depression and uncertainty and failure.

Men's hearts fail them because they are unaware of their relation to the Divine. They think that their life depends upon *matter*. They forget that "the earth is the Lord's, and and the fulness thereof." They do not know the Source of life. They do not know themselves. They see themselves as creatures of circumstance, as mere material beings, as specks in the great cosmos. They become stampeded and subject to heart failure.

It is the office of the healer to call men to *remembrance;* to inspire them with the truth of their Source; to lead them to see the Divine in which they live and move and have their being, of which they live and move and have their being, and because of which they live and move and have their being. God is All, and beside Him there is none else — only God. God is Life, and His Life is the light of men.

When man can know that, he will become luminous and radiant again. The light will come back into his eye, and that light will scintillate through his blood. His heart, having been set right by his knowledge of who he is and what he is, will be strong. He will be restored to his sense of union with the Source of life, which will bring him a new radiance. He will not be depending upon money, or any outer thing; and so he will not be depressed or bowed down or lifeless or suffering from nervous prostration, heart failure, or ennui. He will be potent with life, radiant, glowing, strong with the Love of God, and shining with the God Light. He will walk again in the consciousness of his strength and power and majesty as a son of God.

When we can see that we are constituted of the Essence of God and can realize our sonship to the Most High, we shall find a new element, as it were, entering into the blood stream. The blood will take on another consistency. It will respond differently to the various chemical agents than it formerly did. It will be vital with a new force. We will detect a new power within us — the power of the pure Light of God. Man is the recipient of that transfiguring Power of God. Man is the custodian of it. It is God in action, the living Essence, the living Breath of man's being.

We live because God is Life. We are the manifestation of God. When we become *really* conscious of this, we shall find that the Life which is Light will scintillate through our arteries and through our veins. Our flesh will be luminous and vital with the beauty and strength of the Divine Life. We will know our relationship to God; we will *know* that we are the sons of God.

So for a case of heart trouble, get back to the Root of being, the central Truth, to the great fact that God is All and in all, and beside Him there is none else. There is nothing but God in the whole universe. The universe is a vesture of the Divine One. There is no matter, no material world, no material man.

Man is the radiant child of God, who is Spirit. Man is spiritual, the universe is spiritual, the world is spiritual. The laws that govern man's being are the laws of the Spirit of Life. If you, as the healer, can realize that, your so-called patient will never again be deceived into having heart trouble. He will be praising God for the goodness of his life.

"For the law of the Spirit of life in Christ Jesus hath made me free from the law of sin and death," declared Paul. He had seen in the Invisible that which Peter and James and John had been given to see in the flesh — the radiant Life of the Spirit, bodily, in Christ Jesus. On the Mount of Transfiguration, Jesus appeared to them as He really was; "and His face did shine as the sun, and His raiment was white as the light." He showed them the Word of Truth, that Word which He had spoken when He said: "I am the light of the world." "Ye are the light of the world." "Where I am, there ye may be also." "Follow Me."

Know ye not that ye are the children of Light? If you can know that Truth, you can speak the word of Truth, the word that awakens man to a sense of who he is and what he is and establishes his consciousness in true relation to his Source. With that quickened consciousness he will out-picture the Truth of his being; he will show forth outwardly the health and the strength that is his.

God is Life, and that Life in man is the Light of man, making him a luminous, intelligent being. It is the Light which quickens his intelligence and inspires it with higher understanding and greater wisdom.

When man's quickened understanding begins to manifest, it shows itself through his eyes. His eyes show forth light, and that light is life and strength; so they show life and strength and harmony and order. When man is awakened to see and know the Truth, when he abides in the Truth, keeping his vision undiverted and his thought unswerving, his eyes take on a new focus. They become supple and elastic, and the astigmatism and false focusing disappear, for these conditions come from trying to look in several ways at once. But by singleness of vision and thought, the weak muscles of the eyes become strengthened, coordinated, balanced, and synchronized.

All sickness is the result of harboring mistaken ideas, of forgetting the Truth of our being. We must be reminded of who we are, of our oneness with the Truth — our relationship with God. We must be called back into giving constant attention to our Source. As we live in constant remembrance, we have revealed to us the secrets of the Divine Nature.

Then, as we understand God more and more, we shall know ourselves; and, knowing ourselves, we shall express God. Knowing ourselves as children of the Light, we shall shed the Light. We shall be radiant with that Light. We shall be strong and vibrant with the activity of that Light and with the consciousness of Life. As we grow more and more familiar with the Truth, we find that the Light becomes brighter and more vibrant.

You undoubtedly know that, in physics, the higher a force is raised, the more potent it is and the more easily it works. But there are forces of such high character, of such fine and subtle quality, that we have no instruments for them, and these are the most potent forces in the world.

As our consciousness rises to the One Power, as we acknowledge that One Power and feel our union with It, we shall know these higher, finer potencies and shall ourselves become the instruments of their expression — their radioactive energy. They have the effect in man's soul of calling or drawing him back to his Source. They quicken the hunger in him until he turns away from the husks of material thinking and getting, and remembers his Father. "Blessed are they which do hunger and thirst after righteousness: for they shall be filled."

The call of these infinite potencies of tne Spirit makes man homesick. When he gets very homesick, he will turn toward his home; and his home is in God. Man's home is Heaven. We are strangers in the outer world — the world of our imaginations and untrue experiences.

But when we shall see the truth of our Source and know our divine nature in its oneness with God, we shall be strangers to all our old beliefs, ideas, and thoughts. We shall have a new concept of ourselves and a new understanding of That which gives us life and upon which we depend. For when we turn to the Source and have become acquainted with Its Nature and Its mode of action, we shall find It to be

Love — the Love that is God. God is Love. God's whole Law is a Law of Love, and His Power is the Power of Love.

When the Divine expresses Itself in the earthly state of mind, it quickens the intelligence. There is nothing that can quicken the perception of the mind so much as to know one's relation to the Source, to know that God is the Source, to know that God is Life, that God is Spirit, that God is Love. It makes the mind brilliant. It quickens the intellectual faculties and gives them a new incisiveness, a new sensitiveness, a new power of penetration and comprehension, so that these faculties become illumined and enabled to discern the Truth. The mind will be quick to recognize things that it had looked upon before but had not seen. A new world will open up to our divinely quickened mind, right where we stand.

We do not have to run to and fro over the earth seeking supply or freedom. "The Kingdom of Heaven is at hand." The Kingdom of Heaven is the infinite Realm of the Free Spirit. It is the Kingdom of Life and Light. When we are aware of Life and Light, we shall also be aware of health and wholeness and peace and joy. We shall find that harmony which the Life and Light of God have established within the mind and body of man.

But, as I have said, it is unwise and unprofitable to concern ourselves with the body. We will understand it better than do the hygienists or the physiologists or the chemists, because we will see what they cannot see. We will see through the body. It will be luminous and radiant and entirely transparent to the eye that is lighted with the Light of Truth.

Jesus understood the body perfectly. Do you not believe that? He knew all there is to know about anatomy and physiology and chemistry; yet He never studied any of these things. For it is not the knowledge of the body that heals the body. No chemist, no physiologist, no doctor of medicine, has ever done those things which are recorded of Jesus. None of them has ever done that work. It cannot be done from that plane of knowledge. It is the Light that comes from above that gives us the true insight which sees man as he *is*. This is the true knowledge and therefore the true healing power.

We shall see man as he is because we have turned to his Source and are watching the Divine; but, I repeat, we shall detect the mental inharmonies because we are so conscious of the Divine Harmony. We shall be like the musician who is so sensitive to the nature of music that he immediately senses the slightest falsity; but knowing that the discords do not affect the principle of music in any way, he pays no attention to them and never deviates from knowing the true and the right.

So we, not by studying abnormal or pathological states, but by not believing them nor concerning ourselves with them, shall keep our eye single in our knowing of the True and the Real. We shall keep our heart in the Heart of God. We shall keep our mind *stayed* on the Divine Principle, on the Living Spirit — the Spirit of all life, which is omnipresent, from which we cannot separate ourselves.

As we become truly aware of the Oneness of God, of Him who works through love, of That which no man can describe because It is Spirit and transcendent to the Intellectual processes, so shall we know by an *inward knowing.*

When we touch that inward knowing and see how the Father works through that Spirit of Knowing which is Love, then we lose all fear; we see that there is absolutely nothing to fear, nothing to fight against. For we realize that everything is the product of that Spirit, that there really is no material thing in the universe, that there is no material law or process; but that it is all the action of that Light which is Love and Life and Spirit.

Experience in healing shows us that back of every state of illness there is fear. Back of every state of heart disease there is fear. Do not wrestle with the heart or with any physical or mental condition, but know that "perfect love casteth out fear." He that has fear "is not made perfect in love." We are made perfect in love when we go back to the Source and Foundation of Life — to Love Itself, the Divine.

Our patient will be set free; for in the recognition of our oneness with the Divine Love, we shall understand that all is God, that all is Love. We shall be aware that Love is everywhere roundabout, manifesting Itself in limitless ways; that, indeed, there is no limit. God is omnipresent and God is omnipotent and God is omniscient — the unlimited, limitless ONE.

There is no limit anywhere in God, and His Love moves everywhere. Everywhere we turn, we are facing the evidences of the activity of the Divine Love. When we realize that, our life becomes one of great freedom and joyousness.

We will then realize that every time we sit down to a meal, we are at the communion table. We are in the Presence of God, and we are partaking of the Divine Substance. Even in the so-called earthly food we partake of that Substance. It is all the product of the Light which is Love, which is the Spirit, which is what God *is*.

God is All and in all. So we see that "in Him we live, and move, and have our being." We live *on* Him as well as *in* Him. Everything that we have is the product of the Divine Love.

We are partakers of the Divine Nature, and everything that we do, every act that we perform, is a movement of that Divine Nature, though man has not yet seen and acknowledged this to be true. Man is the son of God, but he does not yet *know* this truth. Every being and every thing is of God, of the Son of God, of the Light of God.

When we see that, we shall understand and know the truth of Paul's words: "There is therefore now no condemnation to them which are in Christ Jesus" — to them who know in whom they live, move, and have being; to them who realize that God is All in all. They will receive "this mind, . . . which was also in Christ Jesus," and radiate consciously the Divine Nature.

The Divine Nature says, "Ye are gods; and all of you are children of the Most High." The Divine Spirit calls us to remembrance. Let us remember! Let us fill our minds again and again with the truth that God is All. Let us know that there is no being, no presence, no power, no intelligence, no life, and no love but GOD. God is ALL.

## LESSON V

ONE of the matters from which we need healing is the sense of want. Everywhere men seem to be bound to their sense of want. The world is in that state of mind. Whole countries are in a condition of poverty or in a state of fear toward that condition. People everywhere are talking about what they call the depression or the recession or the economic problem.

They talk about it and thereby they magnify it. They are watching need, want, lack, deprivation, and negation; and their conversation shows where their vision is set. The experts also, in their talk about economics, keep their attention toward need and want and unemployment. They are trying to devise ways and means of overcoming these things.

But there are no such things to overcome. There is no lack, no absence of plenty, to overcome. If you look around, you will notice that there is really no lack anywhere. There is no want of anything. Even if you look with your so-called material eyes, you will find that there is no scarcity of anything.

You may say that people are going hungry. You may say that there is a need of food. But if you inquire into the subject, you will find that there is more food right now in the country and in the world than we can possibly eat. There is no want of food.

You may say that people are without sufficient clothing,

and that there is a great need of clothing. There is not any such need, for there is more clothing already made up than we can wear. The manufacturers have so much clothing on hand that they do not know what to do about it. Nor do we need shoes. There are already more shoes than we need. The shoemakers do not know what to do about their surplus shoes, they have so many right now.

We might go through the whole list of the articles and things we commonly use, and we would find that there is no need anywhere if we look at the things themselves. We have more things now than we can possibly use, and yet people are saying that there is a lack of everything. There is not the slightest insufficiency anywhere. On the contrary, there is abundance and to spare.

The people who think and talk of lack are dealing in falsities. They are saying that which is not so. That which is not so is a lie. "All men are liars," said the Psalmist. For although God made man to be a witnesser of the Truth and a speaker of It, yet men and women all over the world are stating untruths most of the time. They are not doing the Will of the Father. They are lying, for they are talking about things that are not so.

Therefore the healer, who is steadfastly a witnesser of the Truth, follows Paul's wise admonition to "let God be true, but every man a liar." Thus he is not led astray, out of sympathy, to believe or listen to any of the lies that he hears. He perceives the lie and the liar, but he banishes them out of consciousness.

That is what healing is. To use a common expression,

healing is "nailing a lie." This means that the healing word exposes the lie *as a lie*. The healer silently states that a false belief is a lie and makes it known as a lie. When a thing is known as a lie, it loses its grip upon us. It no longer affects us. We do not believe it. We see that it is not anything, never was and never will be anything; and so we are free of it.

The statements of lack which people are making are statements of non-truth, and they are lies. They should be understood as such and not accepted. It is the acceptance of a lie that hurts. The lie itself does not hurt. It does not have any power to hurt. There is no intelligence or force or substance or will or objective in a lie. It is just so much nothingness. When we do what is called "nailing a lie," we are uncovering the nothingness of it and making men see that nothingness.

It is the *belief* in the lie that hurts; so the hurt is always in ourselves. We hurt ourselves by believing that which is not true. The thing itself does not hurt us. It does not have any power to hurt. The power is all in ourselves. When we realize what it is that hurts us, we will not lay waste our power by believing in lack. We will turn away from the nothingness of lies.

There is really no absence of anything needful in the world. If we will simply see and know the *presence* and plenty of everything that we need, we shall free ourselves from the sense of want and bondage; and our own knowing will be contagious. We shall be the means of freeing others. For healing is largely a matter of contagion. We have used that word as though its meaning were appropriate only to disease and undesirable conditions. We have linked it in our minds with pathological states. But *contagion* is a perfectly legitimate word in relation to good. There is a contagion of peace and joy, of happiness and serenity. There is a contagion of the sense of opulence and bounty.

We always carry around with us some sort of contagion. Most people today are walking in the belief in lack — lack of all the so-called necessities of life. Because they entertain that feeling of lack in their consciousness, they carry about with them that sort of contagion. Their world catches and reflects their consciousness. It conforms to their belief. Then the whole world seems like their own consciousness, because it gives back to them the results of their belief. They are reaping what they have sown.

But what they feel and what they believe is not true. They are walking in a state of false belief, in a semi-hypnoidal state of mind. They are walking in a partial sleep. The idea of want which they carry about with them sheds a contagion of fear, which, in turn, tends to hold other people in the spell of want. There is no want. There is no truth in their idea. It is all a belief in their minds. But the world is to each person according to his consciousness.

There is no need or absence of good anywhere. Even in the so-called material way of seeing things, one finds no absence of anything that is needful to human welfare. All over the earth there is plenty of everything. The idea of depression and want is pure imagination.

When people use their imagining power in a false way, they build around themselves what we call a vicious circle — a circle of thought which circumscribes and encloses them, to which their minds react until they feel that it is real. That is a vicious circle, and it is also called hell.

The word *hell* is a perfectly good old English word. It means to circumscribe, to limit, to bind. We do not like to use that word, but it is often heard in England, especially in the rural districts. When the English farmer puts his stock within an enclosure, he speaks of "helling it," or of putting it in hell. When he separates the young stock at the time of weaning and puts it in a corral, he is *helling* it. To put animals in an enclosure which limits all their movements and deprives them of freedom is to put them in hell. That is the real meaning of the word.

But mankind is not put in hell by some superior intelligence. Man puts himself in that state of mind by his own belief in things that are not of the Spirit. Many of us have felt ourselves to be in hell, to be held. When we speak of being tied up or held, we are using the verb of *hell*. We are helling ourselves. We think we are limited, that we cannot express ourselves, that we are not free.

If you have ever been in the cow country among the cowboys, you have seen their ponies stand for a long time, all day sometimes, with the reins free but hanging down in front of them and touching the ground. The ponies have been trained to believe that when the reins are in that position they are fastened to something. All the cowboy has to do is to drop the reins on the ground and that pony is sure that he is tethered and cannot move. He will not attempt to move. Of if he does, he will just circle around the reins, but he will not attempt to move away from that one spot.

He is perfectly free actually; yet he is not free because he is tethered in his mind.

Thus it is with us. We are tethered by our belief in things that are not so. We are held by the self-imposed feeling that we cannot move. We even put ourselves in dark prisons of false belief and we keep adding to the seeming strength of the walls by thinking and talking about our lack of sunlight and freedom.

We are serving time just now to the lie of imprisonment in lack and deprivation. All this is mere nothingness. The belief is false. It is a lie. We need to awake. The lie is stupefying to the believer. So he who knows the Truth must shake these self-deceived believers out of their stupor. It is really stupid to believe in lack.

But it is especially stupid to say that there is an absence of good when those who say so claim that they believe in God, the All-Good, Omnipresence, Omniscience, Omnipotence. If they believed in the True God, they could hardly say that there was an absence of good anywhere. God is good; He is omnipresent. These people are like houses divided against themselves, and Jesus said that such could not stand.

The world at large is in this condition of contrariness. The country is the expression of its people, and the people are believing in the *absence* of good while they are declaring their belief in the *presence* of it. They pray for good, but their attention is cast toward an absence of something good. They say that God is omnipresent, but they contradict themselves the next moment by descriptions of their neighbor's misfortune or their own poor circumstances. They keep voicing the absence of good because they are judging by appearances and not by righteous judgment. Thus they divide their minds.

They divide their forces; they scatter their powers. Such a state of mind is without a base in consciousness and without a center; and such people wonder why they cannot concentrate. They say they have not the power of concentration. But concentration is not found in division.

Concentration is being centered. It is not the act of focusing on something outside of yourself. It is not being able to stare at a nail in the wall without blinking an eye. Concentration means having a center within, into which you can gather yourself and abide. Concentration is being with a center, having a center, having a base in consciousness from which to operate. It is being aware of the Light within you which you may radiate outwardly wherever you wish.

A good illustration of something that is concentrated may be found in the searchlight which we swing around and play upon different objects. You have seen a searchlight operate. You know that you may play it upon any object you like and leave it there as long as you like; and the longer it rests there, the more you see of that object and the more you understand it.

The concentrated mind is the mind that is based and centered in the Truth. It can swing and play the light around by resting it wherever one's choice may be. This activity does not *bore* into anything; it does not force its way anywhere; there is nothing tense about it. Nor is there any struggle to place the mind. The mind simply rests with the light and turns it where it wishes for as long as it wishes. It is the light itself that brings understanding and draws to you those things upon which you have rested it. You just quietly let them come.

If you are concentrated in the truth that God is All, and confidently believe that God is Omnipresence, Omniscience, Omnipotence, then you are truly based and centered. You stand and walk in the good. Everywhere you are, you are in the midst of good. With the light of that understanding you may look round about, and everywhere that you play the light, the good will move toward you through the light. It will reveal its nature to you and give you of its secrets.

But if you are believing that good is absent, if you are thinking that it is possible for there to be an absence or insufficiency of good, and you are playing your attention around on the external world, saying that this or that good and needful thing is lacking, then you are not centered. You are not concentrated, for you are without a center. You will find yourself being scattered and disintegrated and torn apart.

Concentration is a state of integration. It is a state of being fixed and stable and strong within, and of being conscious of that stability and strength. It is a state of being girded because of having a fixed center in consciousness. The state of concentration is like having a universal pivot upon which you may turn a light in any direction, wherever you will.

If you stand firm in the belief that God is Omniscience, Omnipotence, and Omnipresence; if you are fixed in that understanding; if you realize it and know it as the Truth, then you will find that there is going forth from you a steady light that plays on the good and sees it. Wherever you are, good moves toward you.

Most people are rushing around, hunting for their good. They have an innate feeling that they have a right to good, a right to those things that tend toward happiness, contentment, and satisfaction; but at the same time they feel the absence of them. They have made the mistake of seeking after *things,* and so they are reaching *out* for their good. They plot and plan and scheme and work to get that good, striving to find in outer realms those things which they feel will administer to their peace of mind and to the satisfaction of their physical needs and wants.

The wise men of the East knew better than that. The wise men of all time have known better than that. They have admonished us and taught us and tried to make us see that our good is *at hand.* "Thine own is seeking after thee"; they say, "therefore cease thou from seeking after it."

All that busy, anxious, outward seeking which we do simply shows an absence of understanding on our part and not an absence of our good. Such seeking is quite contrary to the teachings of the wise of all ages and distinctly not in accord with the words of Jesus, the Master, who said, "Seek ye first the kingdom of God, and His righteousness; and all these things shall be added unto you."

When we seek first that Kingdom which is within — the Kingdom of Being, the Kingdom of Knowing, the Kingdom of Feeling — we find that all outer things which are good move toward us. We find that the Light of the Lord actually does stand over us and goes before us. "And the Lord

went before them by day in a pillar of a cloud, to lead them
the way; and by night in a pillar of fire, to give them light;
to go by day and night." We find that every step of the way
is made straight for us and every provision made. We will
not want for any needful good if we seek first the Kingdom
of God.

We all know that sickness is not good. In any of its
forms or symptoms it is not good. Pain is not good, deformities are not good, and disease is not good. None of these
non-goods are of God, and they do not obtain in His Kingdom. They are not present and they are not known in His
Kingdom. To talk to God about sickness and misery and
poverty is just foolishness. It is like trying to convince
God of a lie. You can ignore all these things and simply
seek God. in whom you will find the Truth which is always
good.

It is good to be healthy. It is good to be strong. It is good
to be free from want and limitation. It is good to be poised
and serene, calm and happy and joyous. It is good to be well,
to be at peace within yourself mentally and bodily. That is
your good. That is what will be added unto you if you seek
first the Kingdom of God and His Righteousness.

The true healer always goes to that Kingdom when responding to a call for help. He knows that he is always in
that Kingdom, and that he does not have to treat any being
or condition or circumstance. He has to know only where
he is and what he is and who he is. He is always dealing
with himself, for he is the only patient there is; and even
the healer as the patient is but a way of speaking.

There is no patient in reality. But there is a call for the

lifting up of consciousness. The true healer clarifies his own consciousness from all that may be akin to that outer state which is presented to him, and he knows that there is no power in circumstance or condition. He seeks first the Kingdom of God and His Righteousness, and he abides therein.

"Be still, and know that I am God." Instead of being disturbed by the condition, be still, that you may know the Truth.

The true healer abides "in the secret place of the most High." He is "under the shadow of the Almighty." And he who is overshadowed by the Almighty shall partake of Almightiness, shall receive of that One, and be strong. He partakes of the peace that passes all understanding, and he is at peace. Perfect peace is contagious. If the healer has that peace, the so-called patient catches it.

This matter of contagion is a rather great factor in healing, because we are all in the One Mind. If we are in the right state of consciousness — that is, if we are at one with the Divine Consciousness — then others will feel it, for there is really only the one state of consciousness.

There is just one real, living state of consciousness, because you can hardly say that groping around in beliefs and opinions and feelings about things that are not so is a real state of consciousness.

In healing, we are committing ourselves to that One Real Consciousness, which is of the Wholeness of God — the Almighty, the One Power, the All-peaceful, the All-joyous, the All-wise, the All-intelligent, and the All-good: always and everywhere present.

When we walk in that Presence, we know that wherever we are, we are in that Goodness; It is there. We need not go anywhere to find God, for God is right where we are. He is omnipresent, and we walk in Him. We live and move and have our being in God — the everlasting, unchanging Good. That Good goes not up and down; It is changeless.

The practice of healing is an abiding in the consciousness of the one infinite, eternal Mind, "with whom is no variableness, neither shadow of turning."

As the healer abides in the unchanging Truth, the change in appearances takes place automatically. "I will make darkness light before them, and crooked things straight," says the Lord.

"Thou shalt also decree a thing, and it shall be established unto thee." How do you decree a thing? You decree it by declaring it to be already so. "Declare thou, that thou mayest be justified," said the Voice of the Spirit to Isaiah.

What shall you declare?

"Put Me in remembrance," says the Word of God. "Remember ye not the former things, neither consider the things of old. Behold, I will do a new thing; now it shall spring forth; shall ye not know it? I will even make a way in the wilderness, and rivers in the desert."

You declare the Truth. A declaration of the Allness of God — the Presence of His Peace and Power and Joy and Strength — enforces your awareness that His Kingdom is established unto you. You do not wrestle with disease or aches or pains. It is not necessary. There is nothing to them. There is nothing in them. God never created them, and they do not belong in His Kingdom. Why wrestle with them? Why try to know anything about these things which are not so? They are false and untrue. They have no real being, no substance, no power, no force, no objective.

"Acquaint now thyself with Him, and be at peace: thereby good shall come unto thee," said the seer of old. Only good shall come to you when you acquaint yourself with the Divine One and are at peace. When you are walking in that true sense of peace, no turmoil of thought, emotion, or circumstance shall disturb you or make you afraid.

"None of these things move me," said Paul. He was poised, serene, concentrated, in singleness of mind toward the One. He had touched the basis of the Divine Peace when he said, "I know whom I have believed." — "I *know.*"

The healer is a knower, and he stands firm in his knowing. That is all he has to do. *I know in whom I believe. I am not speculating. I am not philosophizing or wondering. I know.* We have to pass into that state wherein we know, wherein we feel; for healing is not done in the mind nor by the powers of the intellect; it is done in the heart. It is done through the feeling, through the heart's realization of Truth.

When we feel the reality of the Truth in our hearts, we know it in our minds, in our souls, in our strength, in our bones, and throughout the depths as well as the heights of our consciousness. And when we know like that, our so-called patients feel it and get well. We do not have to watch them getting well. They were well already; and we already knew it.

As healers we must seek first the Kingdom of God. We must touch that central, secret place of the Most High and keep ourselves in that state of consciousness which Jesus called "the Kingdom of God . . . within you."

When we dwell and abide and stand firm in that One Consciousness, we shall find that the silent word going forth from us is not without power. On the contrary, anything and everything we do will have in it the power of the Spirit. Yet we do not do things. We feel and know and let it be done.

Jesus went about among the people, and they were healed. There was a contagion of wholesomeness and joy all around Him that went forth from Him and was operative everywhere. It was because of what He *knew*, and because of where He was. "Where I am, ye may be also," He said. "He that believeth on Me, the works that I do shall he do also." But though the visible Jesus was called good, He Himself knew that there is only one Good, which is God; and He pointed the attention of others toward That One.

"Acquaint now thyself with Him." Know Him. Walk with Him. Be aware of His Presence in you and all around you. Then you will find that all good moves toward you, and that there is no lack of anything that tends toward your welfare, your happiness, and your satisfaction. You shall not want for any outward thing that is needful for your service to mankind; for when you have touched the Kingdom of God, you have touched the Kingdom of the Great Servitor of the universe. Jesus called Him *Father*.

The father is always a servant. The father of a family is the servant of the whole family. He works for them, provides for them, cares for them — in a word, serves them. How much more shall your Heavenly Father, "of whom the whole family in heaven and earth is named," serve you, His children, as well as that vast universe which He created. "I have made, and I will bear; even I will carry, and will deliver you."

God the Almighty is the supreme, universal Servant. Jesus Christ came to do the Will of the Almighty, the pleasure of the Father, saying, "I am among you as He that serveth." The Son of God came into the world, not to be ministered unto but to minister. "Whosoever will be great among you, shall be your minister: and whosoever of you will be the chiefest, shall be servant of all."

Who is the greatest among you? It is always the High I Am, God Almighty, the One and Only Good, which is more willing to give than you are to receive. Let Him be your Servant, and He will serve you.

If you think you have to plead and struggle to get what you need, you are asking amiss. Your right asking is your understanding of God's Presence, God's Givingness, God's Kingdom. Jesus, in His understanding of the Divine Nature, simply "gave thanks," and it was done unto Him according to the Perfect Will of the Father. "Use not vain repetitions, as the heathen do": He said, "for they think that they shall be heard for their much speaking. Be not ye therefore like unto them: for your Father knoweth what things ye have need of, before ye ask Him."

You who have been parents, wise parents, knew what your children would need long before they ever thought of it. Gladly and lovingly you had it already provided when the time came for them to have it and use it. You saw to it that when they needed something, it was right at hand for them.

You yourselves are children of God. Your Heavenly Father knows. God is Love, and Love is always giving. "No good thing will He withhold from them that walk uprightly," says the Psalmist. And we know that to walk uprightly is to love God. Also, He has already given us that love with which to love Him, for, as John truly tells us, "We love Him, because He first loved us."

When we feel that Divine Presence and know that It operates through the Principle of Love, which is always outgoing and giving and bestowing, then instead of striving and straining and begging for what we need, we shall find that all good is present, at hand, moving toward us and seeking us.

Do not seek things, but "seek ye first the Kingdom of God, and His righteousness; and all these things shall be added unto you."

"The wind bloweth where it listeth, and thou hearest the sound thereof, but canst not tell whence it cometh, and whither it goeth: so is every one that is born of the Spirit." So are they that are borne with the free wings of the Free Spirit. They are not fettered nor bound nor circumscribed. They are not deprived of any needful good, for all things are added unto them.

If you are teachers and healers, and have touched that Kingdom which we are talking about, I am simply telling you that which you already know. But reiteration is good for us. We need to be reminded of the Truth because we allow our vision to be caught by appearances, and sometimes we allow our judgment to be warped by them. We forget the admonition of the Great Teacher: "Judge not according to the appearance."

Do not let the appearances roundabout you influence or affect you. Judge not by the outer, but "judge righteous judgment." Keep your eye single, and your body shall be full of light. You shall be free and healthy and strong, and the way shall be made straight before you. Bring yourself back often, and return to the Almighty, that you may be more and more conscious of the rest and peace and joy and satisfaction that is of the Kingdom.

When we dwell in the consciousness of the Kingdom within us, and think only of those things that are of the Spirit, all outer things do readily conform and shape themselves for us. The entire universe administers to our good, reinforcing our true consciousness and adding those material things, so-called, which the world calls good.

So shall we be served, and so shall we serve others. For we are here to serve. "Freely ye have received, freely give," said Jesus to His disciples. We shall not want for anything that will augment our powers and be of service to us, that we may, in turn, increase our service to others.

The healer ministers to others when he gives his service to the Most High One. So does the Spirit baptize and inspire and ordain him through all his selfless knowing and living and speaking of the Truth.

# LESSON VI

THERE are many students of the healing art who are working on the plane of thought and belief, and so their minds are still doubtful as to where to put their attention in healing. "Should we hold the suffering and discord in mind," they ask, "when we enter into the place of Silence for the purpose of dissolving these falsities? Should we think of the patient and see him as a personality, as an individual; or are we to look at some other object? Exactly where is the attention of the healer to be placed?"

If you have studied and practiced the preceding lessons, you may be shocked that such questions could be asked; but it is well to answer them thoroughly for ourselves and others so that the idea behind them may be uprooted entirely, lest we be caught in a like mistake sometime when we are trying to heal. So let us remember and repeat the principle of healing until we have learned the simple, straight way and can walk in it without deviation toward outer occurrences, appearances, or objects.

The answer to these questions is always the same. In healing we give our attention wholly to the Truth. We do not hold any person or any thing in mind. We ignore the condition and we ignore the patient. We turn to the Divine, to God, to the Kingdom of God, wherein there are none of these things which we have been asked to heal. We enter the Kingdom of Peace, wherein no discord or inharmony or disease obtains. We forget the objective world, in which no two people agree or see a thing alike.

When you are engaged in healing, it is because you have been drawn into it by the Spirit; but before you entered upon the practice of healing, there had been some inner urge that drew you into that ministry. It is a high calling, and those who are really in it are in the Heights. They live in the Presence of the Divine. They know God, who is Love.

"No man hath seen God at any time. If we love one another, God dwelleth in us, and His Love is perfected in us. . . . And this commandment have we from Him, That he who loveth God love his brother also." And in this same epistle John warns us, "He that loveth not his brother abideth in death. . . . If a man say, I love God, and hateth his brother, he is a liar: for he that loveth not his brother whom he hath seen, how can he love God whom he hath not seen?"

The true healer abides in Life, which is Love. He is awake and alive in Love. If one has not that love for his fellow-men that he should have, he should not go into the ministry of healing or try to heal, because healing is of the Spirit of God — and God is Love. If one's heart is not inspired with love for one's fellow-men, one is not called of the Spirit.

Those who are engaged in healing, if they are successful, are lovers of God and lovers of man. They have the spirit of the commandment that Jesus, the Master, declared unto us: "Thou shalt love the Lord thy God with all thy heart, and with all thy soul, and with all thy mind. This is the first and great commandment. And the second is like unto it, Thou shalt love thy neighbor as thyself." These two commandments embody all the law. "Love is the fulfilling of the law."

It is pure love that makes the connection between you and your patient, and not the attention of your mind toward him. If a patient comes to you for healing, in confidence that you can be of service, you answer that call because you are urged by the Spirit of Love — the Spirit of God which serves. "I am among you as He that serveth," said Jesus.

"And whosoever of you will be the chiefest, shall be servant of all. For even the Son of man came not to be ministered unto, but to minister, and to give His life a ransom for many." The more you give your life to that Divine Love, the more successful will be your ministry of healing.

In responding to a call for help, you respond because you love to serve, you love to do good. You say to whoever asks of you, "I will help, I will heal," or words to that effect. Then that statement — and the thought that prompts it — is your connection with your so-called patient.

The patient has appealed to you, and your willing response has established your *rapport* with him. That is all that needs to be done in regard to persons. It was the Father in you that caused the person to ask for help, and it was your love of serving that caused you to respond. In that agreement, as it were, between you and your patient, there has been established a concord of giving and receiving; and after this is established, you can no longer think of your patient. Your agreement with him has been recognized in the Kingdom of Heaven. It is on the plane of Love. It is on the plane of God. It is in the Spirit. Now you may forget the individual and remember that it is the Father that does His Work.

You are not treating the individual. You are not treating a person. The individual who has appealed to you has become the victim of some psychic fixation; he is apparently suffering from some false belief; and you are to dissolve that falsity. It is destroyed just as light destroys darkness. If you want to remove darkness from a room, you do so by establishing light. You do not concern yourself with the darkness; you concern yourself with the light. You turn on the light and maintain it.

Disease is a state of darkness, and in order to remove that darkness you, so to speak, turn on the light of health. Disease is a falsity; and to banish it, you establish yourself in the Truth, and the Truth dispels the falsity. It cannot stand in the presence of Truth, any more than darkness can remain in the presence of light. Light never touches darkness, because darkness is nothing. There is nothing to touch. Light does not dispel darkness by taking hold of it — by handling it. Light simply stands and is radiant with its own glory.

In spiritual healing, you are not concerned with the so-called disease, the negation, the falsity, the error, the discord. You are interested in harmony and truth and righteousness and peace and health and wholeness — all those things that constitute the Kingdom of God. Your attention is on the Kingdom of God. Your attention is not on the falseness and error of the condition, nor is it on the one who is suffering. It is on the Truth Itself. You look to the Truth, and you abide in the Truth. "Ye shall know the Truth, and the Truth shall make you free."

The healer turns his attention to the Truth, and he keeps

it there. He abides in the Truth — not in falsity, not in personality, not in individuality, but in the Truth. He knows the Truth, and that is all he knows.

If the healer turns to the individual, he is looking at the personality; and he will be looking at that personality through the eyes of his own personality. So long as he concerns himself with personality he is going to be drawn down, in some measure, to the level of that personal consciousness. All unwittingly, he will take it on; and to the degree that he does so, he will be frustrated in his efforts to heal. He will not be able to free the individual. He must concern himself with the Truth Itself; and the Truth is impersonal. It has nothing to do with persons.

But all Truth is One Truth. If the individual who is doing the work is in the Truth and conscious of the Truth, the same One Truth in the patient always responds. When the Truth is operative in the consciousness of the healer, it becomes operative in the patient through that hidden light of understanding which is within him.

This is an inner process, a spiritual process. It is not of the intellect nor of the conscious mind, but takes place on a higher plane and through a deeper avenue of being. That which is done, is done because of that which is known by the inner mind in secret, through the heart, through the feeling; "and thy Father which seeth in secret shall reward thee openly." The first thing the healer does is to acquaint himself with God, to commune with the Father "which is in secret," to know the Truth that is in his heart.

"Acquaint now thyself with Him, and be at peace." "Be

still, and know that I am God." Abide in that acquaintance.
Abide in that stillness. Abide in the Kingdom of God. Abide
in God Himself.

If you will ignore personality, you can become so conscious of God that you will lose all sense of personality.
You will not be aware that there is 'any person present in
·all the world. If you get quite away from all personality,
you will get away from your own personality. You will not
know that your own outer self is present. You will become
thoroughly unconscious of your outer person. There will be
no person anywhere, either patient or yourself, as we speak
of persons. You will be completely losing yourself in the
consciousness of the One Presence, the One Power, the One
Intelligence.

Should you become totally absorbed in the Divine to the
utter forgetfulness of all personality including yourself, the
result would be an instantaneous healing. For you would
have entered into that Realm of Absolute Perfection which
is God; and in that Realm of Perfection there can be no
imperfection. In the presence of light no darkness can obtain — it simply is not there. Not that the light is concerned with the darkness; but being light, it is radiant, and
in that radiance there can be no darkness. In the Light of
Truth, in the Radiance of the Glory of Truth, there can be
no disease, no inharmony, no ache or pain or suffering. As
healers we must ignore personality.

You ignore the person, as such, who comes to see you
for treatment, and your attitude is just the same in regard
to the personality of some one far away who has written or
telegraphed to you for help and treatment. In his mind he

has turned to you, and on receipt of his message you turn to him. With the desire to help him you say, "Yes, I will help that person." You have now made an agreement to serve, and that agreement establishes you *en rapport* with that person so far as personality is concerned. Then you will immediately turn to the Realm of Truth, because there is no space, no distance, no time in the Truth.

It makes no difference whether a person is in your presence bodily or whether he is ten thousand miles away. In Spirit there is no time or space. Spirit is timeless and spaceless, because Spirit is omnipresent. When you consciously touch the Presence in one place, you have touched It in the whole universe; for the Presence of the Spirit is that One whose center is everywhere and whose circumference is nowhere. When you realize the Presence of God, you touch Omnipresence. The I Am That I Am is omnipresent. If you have acquainted yourself with the impersonal I Am within you, you will touch the I Am that is present everywhere.

You are not at all concerned with time or space. You do not have to sit and try to shoot your mind to others and see if you can think of them. Some people try to treat that way. They say that they are "going out in love" to this or that person. You cannot go out anywhere, for there is not any "where" in the Spirit. Because the Spirit is everywhere, there is no *where* in regard to the Spirit. The Presence of the Spirit is That which is always *here*. You do not go out to a patient. You go into God, who is right here. God is the Omni-Presence, the Omni-Center. Therefore you will touch your patient through Him, right here in your own consciousness.

You are not dealing with space or materiality or human form when you are healing. You are working in the Formless. Spirit is formless. You are working in, or surrendering your consciousness to, the formless, impersonal, absolute Spirit. If you have merged your consciousness into the Divine Consciousness, your word of Truth — or true self-knowledge — will be active omnipresently; and that word will be felt by your patient wherever he may be.

We speak of God as being the Most High, the Most Within, and the Center of all. This sounds as if the way of God had to do with space, but that is not so. I will give you an illustration of what "most high" means in the science of radio, and it will also appear to be spatial; but you may translate your hearing of it into an inward perception of inner things. Of course, when we use external comparisons, we are dealing crudely with spiritual verities; and even our most exalted descriptions of the ways of God are but figures of speech. But the following story may help you to understand more clearly the principle of touching the Most High in healing.

Some years ago, there was a storm on the Atlantic. The wind had reached a gale velocity, and there were great tidal waves along the coast. It was dangerous to shipping, and the government was trying to send word out to the ships at sea so that they would not attempt to make port or risk being grounded by the raging storm close to shore. Meanwhile, from the ships themselves which had been caught in the storm, there was being sent shoreward a stream of radio cries for help and direction.

Now the government had a tremendous radio station, at that time the largest in the world, and the operators were sending out explicit directions with all the power of that station to all the ships at sea. But their directions did not get to the ships, nor did they receive any of the distress signals which were coming from the ships. Yet the government operators knew what was going on at sea; for they were getting messages — not from the ships, but from another radio station.

There was another radio station that was getting all the messages from the ships and passing them on. The government operators recognized that their own messages were not arriving at their destination but were being retransmitted from some other station which was in perfect communication with the ships. So they asked this unknown station, "Where are you? Who are you?"

The answer came back, "I am a boy, fourteen years old. I am over in Jersey City."

"How is it that you are getting the messages to and from the ships when we cannot do it? What are you operating with?"

"I have a little set of my own. I rigged it up myself."

"You mean you have a little homemade affair, and you are succeeding where we have failed! How do you do it?"

The boy answered, "You are sending out your waves horizontally, and I am sending mine perpendicularly. If I can strike a perfect perpendicular, I can touch eternity."

Thus "out of the mouth of babes and sucklings" is wisdom spoken. Out of the understanding of a little boy, fourteen years old, came the word that changed the whole science of radio transmission; for he had proved the truth of it. His messages got there; while the great, strong radio station of the government had sent out its messages in vain.

However, in healing, you are not sending any messages to any person, either here or there. You are communing with the Spirit. But if your attention is upward unto Eternity, instead of outward unto personality, if you are aware not of persons but of God, and if you have touched His Spirit with your upward watching, then the person will get the word. The God in him will get it. The God in you and the God in him is One God. There is only One God.

That is the answer to the question of where to place your attention in healing. Is it clear and understandable now? God is One God. God is the Omnipresent Presence. If you touch the Presence here in your own consciousness, you touch that Presence everywhere. It is not the person, the patient, that hears and responds; it is God that hears and responds and heals. The person simply reflects the Divine Freedom.

You are dealing with Truth Itself when you are called upon to heal. Truth is God. God is Truth and He does all things in Truth. He does not do anything in error. In our illustration the government station was working in error, so to speak, and the little boy was working in Truth. Truth worked in him and through the device that he had contrived. There was no respect of persons. It was just that

Truth works through the instrument, or channel, which is set toward Itself.

If you set your consciousness toward the Truth, acquaint yourself with the Truth, and are interested only in the Truth, your so-called patient — your ship in distress — will receive your word. He will get the message of Truth direct from the Truth; and he will get it deep down inside: not on the surface, with his senses, nor in his body, but in the innermost of his consciousness. He will feel it in the secret center of his consciousness, and it will well up in him and work out and transform him.

He will be transformed by the renewing of his mind, which you know is the One Mind. Being renewed in the Mind of God — the Spirit — he will be freed of his false beliefs. They will cease to operate. The fears will be allayed, and the false concepts will be dissolved in the Light of Truth. When the imagination is cleared of false concepts, the body, which is the picturing-forth of the mind, will change.

"Be ye transformed by the renewing of your mind" — in the spirit of your mind — by having that Mind in you which was in Christ Jesus. The patient catches the Light of Truth. The Truth in him responds to the Truth in you, because there is only One Truth. You are not *en·rapport* with his body or his mind, but with his Spirit. You do not consider his personality, but your Spirit bears witness to the Spirit in him — that he is the son of God.

The Spirit in you and the Spirit in him is One Spirit and has, of course, no disease. It is immune, immaculate, pure. It is Life. It is pure Light. Darkness never affects light.

The Truth is not affected by the error; but the error, the falsity, is affected by the Truth. It is dispelled by the Truth, as darkness is dispelled by light. We are told to "walk in the light." We are told, "Let your light so shine before men." They, seeing your good works, will not glorify you, but will glorify the Light, the Father of lights, in whom there is no shadow.

You will notice that Jesus, in treating Lazarus, paid no attention to Lazarus. But He did pay attention to God. He renewed and quickened and intensified His own consciousness of the Presence of God, who is all Life and in whom there is no death. Jesus acquainted Himself with God. He found His conscious oneness with the Father. In that oneness of consciousness, He felt Himself sustained and reinforced by God — His own Spirit given additional power, as it were, by the whole Power of the Source of Life. "My Father is greater than I."

At the grave of Lazarus, Jesus knew that the Father was backing up His word of Truth. He knew that the God in Him was one with the God of all universes, the same One God in Him and in Lazarus and everywhere, in all that is. "Father, I thank Thee that Thou hast heard Me," Jesus said before He called Lazarus forth. "And I knew that Thou hearest Me always: but because of the people which stand by I said it, that they may believe that Thou hast sent Me." He had purposely delayed His return to Bethany so that the people might see and believe in the Truth of the Son, so that they might know that man is an immortal being.

It was because Jesus had no belief in death, no sense or feeling of death, that His consciousness was completely quickened and raised above the fact that Lazarus had been buried for four days. He had already told His disciples that "our friend Lazarus sleepeth; but I go that I may awake him out of sleep." Lazarus came to life — in our way of speaking — when Jesus spoke to him; but he never was dead.

Man is the son of God; he is a spiritual being, a manifestation of the Living God. He cannot die. "Said I not unto thee that, if thou wouldest believe, thou shouldest see the glory of God?"

In some schools of metaphysics, they speak of "an idea of God," or "an idea in Divine Mind." An idea in the mind is one with the mind, and it does not become separated from the mind when it is expressed. Even the idea which you pass on to other people does not leave you when you impart it to others. You do not take the idea out of your mind and put it into theirs. You can both have it. So it is with God. An idea which comes from the Divine Mind has not been separated from the Divine Mind but is always there in that Mind. You cannot get it out of that Mind.

As an idea of God, man is not projected forth out of God's Mind into separation from His Mind. Though man is the expression of God's idea of Himself, that idea never leaves Him but is always in and of Himself. An idea is of the essence of that which gave it form. The real Self of man is of the very Stuff and Substance that God is. Man is immaculate and deathless as the being that God made, and he has no pain or trouble of any kind.

In the Mind of God there is no error or falsity or sickness or pain. Nor do the ideas in that Mind change from sickness to health. They are perfect always. Therefore, in healing, when you deal with the Truth and are conscious of the Mind of God, you only *seem* to touch and restore the mind of the patient; you only *seem* to touch and dissolve the error.

People, looking on and seeing the transformation, will say, "That person has been healed. He was sick, and now he is well." But you know that there was not anything to heal. You know that there was nothing amiss in the perfect Mind of God, and that His Mind was there in the patient all the time.

The Son of God, the Real Self, was perfect all the time. The whole matter was on the plane of appearances. It had no substance. "Judge not according to the appearance, but judge righteous judgment." Know the Allness of God; know the Oneness of man with God, and dwell in that Oneness. Be conscious of that Oneness and know that the Self of man is the Self of God. There is only one Self, only one I Am, only one Being. God is undividable. There is no separation, no space, no time, however it may seem.

God is omnipresent. God is here. The Kingdom of God is at hand, right here. The Kingdom of God is with men. The Kingdom of God is within you. You are in the Kingdom of God. Within you and about you is all His Peace, Harmony, Purity, Wholeness, Truth, Beauty, Sweetness, Strength, Goodness; and there is no discord or anything that could cause sickness or pain in His Kingdom. There is nothing that could cause trouble in God's Kingdom, and so there is no trouble anywhere. God is the One and Only Power. He

is the Maker of heaven and earth, and His Glory *fills* heaven
and earth.

God is not acquainted with aches and pains. He knows
nothing about them. There is no use in your talking to God
about them, because He does not hear that language. You
do not have to describe error to God, because His eyes are
too pure to behold iniquity. He cannot see it; there will be
no meaning in what you say. You yourself could not respond to something that was not in your consciousness.

But there is that in you which is the son of God, and does
respond to God. As a son of God, you know goodness; you
can recognize the Truth of God. You recognize the fact
that there is no such thing as an ache or a pain in God.
You know that there is nothing in God to cause sickness and
suffering. God is Pure Love, and He is the only Cause. His
Kingdom is governed by Pure Love, and it is a Realm of
Purity and Harmony and Order and Health and Goodness.
There is no discord in God's World, and so there is no discord anywhere.

In healing, you tell the Truth to God. You do not talk
to the person you are supposed to be healing. You lift the
Truth up to God. The word of Truth always goes upward.
It always ascends. When you speak the Truth "in the ascen-
sion," as they say, that word of Truth is "sharper than any
two-edged sword." It cuts to the marrow of the bones, and
penetrates through consciousness to the very foundation of
being.

But the word penetrates and heals only when it is spoken
upward. And by speaking upward, we mean as the divine
speaking to the Divine, the son speaking to the Father.

Then the Father is heard saying "Amen" to the son, and we know that it is done. But we must remember that there is only one I Am, only one Divine Self.

You yourself have no responsibility toward the case. If you think you have, you are wrapped up in your own personality. Jesus said, "The Son can do nothing of himself." If you can do nothing of yourself, why try to do anything for any person? Some people try to "do" persons. They think they are healing, and so they try to do something to a personality, or handle a person in some way. They see a problem, and they begin working on it; and they feel a responsibility toward the person who has presented it to them. They take the problem and the person on their own shoulders, very much as though there were no God present.

You have no responsibility toward the patient, or toward any person. Your problem and duty and responsibility is with yourself and toward the One, that you may abide in the Truth and know the Truth and stand firm in the Truth. That is your only responsibility — to know and be firm toward the Truth in the midst of the seeming untruth.

If you feel any responsibility toward the person or the untrue situation, you will only have given the untruth a boost. You will have made the unreality seem more real. You will then get entangled in the unreality, and for the time being, you will not be able to extricate yourself. You will be caught to some degree in the same personal consciousness as the first victim, and then there will be two of you. You must deal entirely with your own consciousness and never with the other person.

Everyone around Jesus insisted that Lazarus was dead.

Jesus did not argue with them. He did not try to convince
them of the Truth or change their minds in regard to the
situation. He kept Himself about the Father's business,
that they might *see* the Glory of God with their own eyes.
He let them alone. And He did not give His attention to
Lazarus. He turned to God. He was concerned only with
His own conscious union with the Father; and thus with the
increase, through His consciousness, of the Power of the
Spirit.

Jesus was watching Life and ignoring death. His consciousness was raised and quickened and charged with the
dynamic of the Spirit, so that He spoke the word of command to Lazarus with power. Lazarus responded. The
people standing around heard the mighty word. The glorious Light of the Spirit shone forth from Jesus so brightly
that it dissolved the darkness of their minds. Their false
beliefs vanished, and they saw Lazarus come forth *alive*.

Everything is a matter of consciousness. It is not a physical thing that has occurred when you see sickness and disease. It is a disturbance in consciousness. Man is not material. Man's real being is spiritual. His real body is spiritual. So you are not concerned with the physical aspect at
all. You leave that alone. Also, you are not concerned with
the personality; you ignore that. You are concerned only
with the Truth Itself.

Acquaint now thyself with God, and be at peace. If you
are conscious of peace, if you are abiding in that peace
"which passeth all understanding" — that peace which is
indivisible and omnipresent — your patient will become conscious of the Spirit of peace within himself. It will well up

within him, and then his body will be at peace. Many times in healing, that is all you need to know: the Peace of God. You become so alive to that Peace, so conscious of it and filled with it, that all discord and inharmony fade away at once. Your knowing of the Peace of God is often the only medicine you need to give on a case.

You do not wrestle with cases. You do not strive or fight or resist them. You are still, and you know. The Father is Light, and He knows no shadow. He does the work. The Light Itself does the work. You are to do no work. "Come unto Me, . . . and I will give you rest." While you are resting in the Truth, the work will be going on.

When you go into a house where they say that somebody is breathing his last breath, and they are all waiting around for death, you may feel their pain and fear and agony; but in the midst of this, you must be of a firm mind. You must not enter into these feelings at all. Have that Mind in you which was in Christ Jesus. Know that the appearance is not so. Know that it is false, that it is a lie. Say, "This is a lie, and he is a liar," to yourself — not to the patient or to his family.

Fix your mind on the Truth, and the Light of the Truth will drive the darkness away. It will go. Even if the patient is right in front of you at the point of death, according to their way of thinking, do not give him any attention. No matter what they say, do not pay any attention. Then it will go in one ear and out the other, and you will be abiding in the Truth — and the patient will live.

If there is anybody who needs to have his mind stayed on God, it is the healer, because he is continually besieged by all sorts of people with all sorts of claims of suffering. They want to talk about their sickness and diseases. They want to make much of their sad condition so that the healer will be more concerned about it. They challenge him and try to drag him into their own state of consciousness in order to get hold of his sympathy. They think his sympathy will help them.

It is not easy, I admit, to keep free and firm when some of these states of mind assert themselves so positively, and the appearance seems so real. It is not always easy to keep yourself patiently unresponsive and unsympathetic toward somebody who is suffering. Suppose someone, for instance, sticks a huge boil in front of you and says, "Look at it! See how bad it is! Just get a real look at it, and you can imagine how it hurts!" You must not get a real look at it. People want you to imagine how things hurt. But just do not do it. If you want to heal a boil, do not imagine that boil. You might have one yourself if you let your imagination take steady hold of it, for you would be likely to start believing that it was real.

Some people think that you must have a good imagination to heal. The imagination is never good. There is only One Good, which is God. God does not imagine; He knows. You must have no imagination at all in healing. You must give your entire attention to the Absolute Reality. It is not by your imagining health, nor by imagining God, but by *knowing* God — by letting God know Himself in you — that a healing takes place. "Not by might, nor by power, but by My Spirit, saith the Lord."

It always comes back to your having the single eye. "If

. . . thine eye be single, thy whole body shall be full of light." But if you are seeing things that are not true, your body will be full of darkness. The mind will be dark with the untruth, and then the body will be dark also.

To keep the eye single, you have to be firm. Be of a firm mind. "Let there be a firmament in the midst of the waters." When the waters of human emotion and the seeming adversity of circumstances surge up around you as though trying to drag you in, let there be a firmament in the midst of the confusion. A firm mind is single-eyed. If it be divided, it falls.

Set your attention on High. Send your thought-waves upward. Concern yourself with the Most High only, with the Divine Being, with the Divine Perfection, with the Kingdom of Heaven, which is the Kingdom of Harmony and Peace and Joy and Love and Wholeness. Acquaint yourself with Him who is God, beside whom there is none else.

"Thou wilt keep him in perfect peace, whose mind is stayed on Thee."

# LESSON VII

WERE not the healings of Jesus permanent?

The healings of Jesus may have been permanent, but we have no record of how permanent they were. We know that He restored the widow's son to life, but we have no record that he is still living. Jesus brought Lazarus forth from the tomb, but as far as we know, Lazarus decided to go back some time after that. We have Jesus' words of warning to some persons that they were not to tell anybody of their healing. And we have His words to others, warning them not to return to their old habits, lest they fall into a worse state of suffering than before.

We cannot say of Jesus that all His healings were permanent; for we have no assertion on His part, nor any record from others, to that effect. But it is probable that most of His healings were permanent according to what we mean by permanence in this life, and that the ones He healed did not return to their old states as long as they lived.

This question of the permanence of spiritual healing sometimes arises in the experience of those who are called into the healing ministry. The question came to me in regard to a special case; so I will describe the case in detail and thus bring forth the principles of healing from another point of view.

The so-called patient was a married man with children and with a mother living. He had become addicted to drink. At the time the healer took up the case, he was said to be a drunkard, and he had lost his business. Then he was apparently healed. He became a changed man, a new character.

Some years later, his mother passed away, and then he began drinking again. In fact, he got worse than he had been before the healer treated and apparently healed him. The question is "Why was there a return of this trouble? If it was healed, why did it return?"

In the first place, the man was in the drug business, and the statistics of the United States government show that the percentage of drug and liquor addicts is greater in the medical and drug professions than in any other profession or business.

Such occupations as lead the mind to deal entirely with materiality and physicality engender a thorough and constant belief in material power, material suffering, and the physical reality of evil. Those who are in the drug business believe in material remedies, drugs, stimulants, and sedatives, as sources of relief from their sense of overwork, fatigue, nervous exhaustion, or just plain inertia and lack of interest. They think that their remedies have a power of good that counteracts a power of evil.

Then, again, many people are so busy resisting evil that they get tangled up in negative attitudes. They feel depleted, not because of their work but because of their false states of mind and their continual resistance against what they think to be a real evil or menace to their health and efficiency.

The evil is nothing but their own believing; but they do not know this, and so they resort to mild stimulants to make themselves feel better for their work. Sometimes they are given a tonic by the doctor. Then, gradually, their need of a stimulant becomes a habit and their desire for it increases, until finally, for a more immediate effect, they take to alcoholics of a strong nature.

There are even those preaching the Gospel of Christ who often seem to feel that the devil has more power than God. They are working in the name of Jesus who said, "Resist not evil!" But they keep on resisting because they do not understand what those words mean. They are not really aware of the Divine as the One and Only Power; and they are not relying upon that One Power, though they talk about it. Even ministers of the Gospel forget that "I can of mine own self do nothing"; but that through reliance upon the Divine, "all things are possible."

Thus people rely upon artificial stimulants when they feel their energies at an ebb and they form habits of turning to those things. They think that they find relief and satisfaction in them. Many people turn nowadays to smoking, thinking that they get something out of it, that there is a power in it which imparts something to them. Of course that is not true, but they believe it is.

I had two friends who were lawyers, and they were partners. One of them liked his cocktails and his highballs and his toddies. He said that it made him feel good to have a drink before his meals. "But the idea of chewing a weed," he said, "I can't see anything in that. It seems dirty to me, going around sucking a cigar and chewing at it. You know So-and-So (his partner) always has one in his mouth."

But his partner, when I was out with him, would say, "I

get a lot of satisfaction out of this cigar. I like a good cigar. It is good company. But the idea of pouring firewater down your throat is beyond me. I can't see anything in that."

They were each of them living by their own opinions, and those opinions were just notions and prejudices. Many people think that they are living by principles when they are just living by prejudices. They are living by their prejudices and condemning everybody who is not in accord with them.

I have given at some length one of the reasons why a man turns to drink, and especially drawn your attention to the fact that a druggist is among those listed as prone to drink because of handling and taking tonics and stimulants, and then wanting something stronger in its effects. But if the man (whom we are now interested in as an example) had not been a druggist, he would have been sick in some other way. And his healing would not have been permanent; for there were a number of factors in his case which the healer did not reach and eliminate.

Some healers, as I have said before, send out a strong thought to their patients, which acts as a negation of the false idea in the mind of the patient. The idea becomes stilled. It is rendered quiescent. The pressure of a strong thought against an idea constrains it to inactivity for a time. Mental pressure is a psychic force which has much the same effect as pressing down the lid on compressed air. The more the idea in a man's mind is pressed down, the greater will be the reaction when the pressure is off.

The healer, in our case of the drunkard, was probably

also hampered by her own personal thought in regard to drunkenness. The case probably looked to her as something deplorable and real; and she took hold of it as such with all the power of her positive thoughts pressing down upon the weakness, thus clearing up the surface of the matter, but at the same time only hiding the trouble deeper down where it could gather resistance for a rebound. And the rebound came when the man's mother passed on. If the healer had looked entirely to the Truth, if she had abode in the peace that passes understanding and had communed with the Spirit, making no effort of her own, it would have been revealed to her that the root of the man's trouble was back in his mother.

The mother had dominated the man with a strong will all his life. She had never let go of her son. Her grip upon him was not lessened when she passed out of her body. It was a psychic hold that she had upon him. Of course, the man did not know that he was in bondage to his mother. He just felt bound and fettered and overpowered without understanding why, and so he sought freedom and forgetfulness in intoxication.

But the healer should have discovered this undermining factor. She did not take into consideration all the elements involved in the case, and so the treatment which she gave was partial and temporary. The mother was a paralytic because of some lack of joy in her life and an excess of jealousy which she nursed. She died of a stroke, so-called. All the time she was sapping the energies of her son. These primal and predominating elements were not considered by the healer, and so the condition was not eliminated. It returned.

The healer had used her human will to free the man by the power of "true thought." Any use of the human will in treatment is an exercise of psychic pressure which is always more or less hypnotic. The intention may be good; the desire may be good. In this case, there was a keen desire to free that man and establish him in his family as a normal being. But what has been called the "mortal mind" was used, and its work is always interwoven with an element of hypnosis.

We have to be careful not to work with our human minds. So-called "mortal mind" is a subtle instrument. It is an assuming and presuming thing, and often we bring it into play unwittingly, especially if we have been taught the power of thought and suggestion. We are all likely to have read or heard quite a lot about the power of suggestion. Hypnosis has been advocated as a therapeutic agency, but it is never therapeutic. No matter by whom it is advised or by whom it is practiced, it is always damaging. It is bad for the subject of the treatment, and it has a reactionary effect upon the one who engages in it.

You may know that hypnosis has been employed, however unintentionally, whenever you hear a healer say: "I have handled so many cases today that I am tired. I must have some relaxation. I must take a nap. I must have something to refresh me."

If you are ever tired from healing, you are on the wrong track. You are working with your own mind. When you are working with the Spirit, the more cases you handle, the more refreshed you will be, because the Spirit Itself refreshes you. The Spirit is doing the work, not you; and the

Spirit never tires. It is omnipotent. You, in contact with the Spirit, will be filled with that Spirit, and so you will not get in the least tired. If you do, you may know that the human mind is busying itself, and that you have been working from the plane of your own wish and desire, with the power of your human will.

This type of work was what the healer did in the case just described. Her desire to heal was strong. She probably spent a great deal of time on that case and was much concerned over it. She wanted to see the man restored to manhood, that he might be the rightful head of his family and a man among men. All this was good; but, you see, there was a recognition of evil in her attitude.

All through this healer's treatment, there was her seeing of an untruth, her giving strength to liquor, acknowledging materiality, acknowledging a false condition as reality. There was a dealing in the *seeming*, and that seeming became real to her mind. The heart's desire was right, and the wish to relieve was good; but there was that mistake of seeing reality in illusion, the mistake of being caught by the illusion, and accepting and working against it. Much healing is of that nature.

That is why many persons are frustrated and disappointed in their efforts to heal. They see the condition they have been called upon to heal. They feel their responsibility in the matter. The sense of responsibility weighs upon them, and it is an element in the mind that is hurtful to their work because it puts the self in the way of the Spirit.

In spiritual healing, the more you can get out of the way, the more you can be just nothing, as it were, that God may be All in all, the better and quicker and more permanent will the healing be. As I have said before, the best healer is the one who sees nothing to heal, who sees only Reality, only the Divine, only the Truth.

The true healer knows, once and· for all, that untruth is *nothing*, and so he is never concerned with it. He does not try to produce a new condition. He does not try to manifest Truth, or create true conditions in the place of a false state. A true healer does not try to create anything. He knows that Truth is and always was, and that no one can add anything to it or take anything away from it. The patient has not taken anything away from the Truth. It is still there, and nothing needs to be changed. There may seem to be a devilish appearance, but the devil is not there; it is God who is there. Right there where it seems as if there were something else — just the opposite of God — there is only His Presence, His Truth.

If you ever have a feeling that you are doing the work, you will find that underneath this feeling, deep down in the mind, there is a desire to *do* and to be recognized as a *doer*. It is a subtle desire. The sense of *doing* is but a disguised form of pride. It hides your belief that you have attained, that you have power.

There is but One Power. There is nothing for you to attain. The Truth *is* and man *is;* you do not change the real Self of him. Man is as he is. You cannot really touch the individual, because the individual is a spiritual being; and being spiritual, he is immune and immaculate. He is untouched. The real Self of man cannot be touched by human thought.

You are not to treat anyone by your thoughts. You are to know the Truth. When you know the Truth, you recognize the real Self. The shadows flee away, and that real Self shows itself and comes forth. As it does so, you see a transformation. The man is changed; he is a new being. But he is not changed, and he is not new. He is just showing himself. That glorious Self was there all the time. You have not added anything to that Self. You have not wrought a great work. You have just seen the Truth.

In healing, we have to know the non-reality of the whole matter, and rise to the spiritual consciousness, to the realization of the Oneness of God. God is All in all, and beside Him there is none else. There is no presence, no power, no substance, no intelligence, no will, no manifestation, no activity, no force, no energy, but God. It is all and only God.

The recognition of something else will affect your mind with a sense of disturbance, of obligation, and of fear. If these things creep in, they will serve to cloud and adulterate your consciousness, and you will not be a clean avenue for the Holy Spirit — the Spirit of Wholeness, the Whole Spirit — to have Its free way.

If you recognize another presence and power, you are double-minded. In double-mindedness there is disability, and in that state there is no channel for the dynamic of the Spirit. The work is partial or temporary. There is a return of the condition.

The condition does not always return in the same form that it had. The force of the personal will in treatment sometimes changes the physical aspect, so that, later, the thing will crop up and break out in another department of physical expression. Or it may come forth in uncleanliness of mind, temper, nervousness, or melancholy, and not in the physical body. Of course, this return, whatever its aspect, is not *caused* by the healer. It is just that the healing was not complete.

Sometimes, when you have treated a case, there is no recognition or declaration of it on the part of him who has been healed. It is advisable for you to get that declaration from your patient. If he has a sense of complete restoration, it is good for him to say so. He need not shout it from the housetops or peddle it around among the neighbors. But if he tells you, or just tells himself, the good news, it will benefit him.

On the other hand, if you are ever *hurt* by a lack of recognition or acknowledgment, you will block the way of the Spirit through your consciousness. You will find that you are stumbling in the next case you try to heal, and not being very successful. The mind of the healer must be entirely free from personal feelings. He must not harbor any responsibility, or any desire for recognition or acknowledgment of his work. If either responsibility or acclamation is given you, pass it on up to the Father.

"The Father that dwelleth in Me, He doeth the works," said Jesus. "Why callest thou Me good? there is none good but One, that is God." There is only One Doer. The Truth Itself is the Power.

Give to God the power and the glory, and accept none of it for yourself, because the more you can be free from all these little human twists of consciousness, the more pure and selfless a vehicle you will be for the action of the Spirit;

and therefore the more potent will be the expression of the Truth through you and in you and for you. While it may appear to other people that you have done a certain thing, you can know that you have not done it, because there was not anything to *do*.

If you can put yourself entirely out of the way, so that your personality is thoroughly eliminated, you will be healing, apparently, all the time. You will not be trying to heal, nor will you be speaking any word of healing; but you will be healing constantly, day and night. For, when you have put aside the personal self, you are abiding in the Truth constantly; and the Truth constantly does the work. There should be no labor or effort about healing. If there is, you are on the wrong track.

People have often come to me and said, "I have no consciousness of God." They have set up their little mortal selves as gods, and then they wonder why they are not conscious of the Presence of the Spirit. The Spirit is there within them all the time, but they have given their consciousness to themselves. They abide in their own feelings, and so they do not feel God.

That is the trouble with most people — just their own feelings about their own selves. That being the case, they come to tell you of the feelings they have. They want to be healed of their physical discomfort, but they do not realize that the discomfort is due to their own self-feeling. They try to impress you with their condition in all its details and symptoms. They are busy with their sensations, and they want you to be busy with them too. They think it is important to get your interest so that you can feel their feeling. They are wrapped up in self and their own feelings.

If you are free of all personal self and are centered in the Truth, you can free others from themselves. But you cannot allow yourself to be drawn into these things that you see and hear, or let them appear as realities to you. You have to be on the watch. In spiritual matters you have to watch your step, because it is easy to be led off into the contemplation of that which is not so, and to sympathize with that which has no reality.

You remember the saying that came to Isaiah? "Who is blind, but My servant? or deaf, as My messenger that I sent? who is blind as he that is perfect, and blind as the Lord's servant?" You have to keep your eye and your ear single to the Truth, not now and then, but constantly. Then you can maintain  your integrity and poise and serenity, and be a counter-vehicle, so to speak, for the action of the Spirit.

When you abide in Reality and do not see the appearances presented to you, there seems to be a physical healing. That healing is just an appearance. The whole thing is an appearance. It is not real. We speak of the delusions of the senses and say that healing is simply destroying those delusions. But delusions are not real; so how can we destroy them? Yet people seem to be held and bound by delusions and psychic fixations. When they are pictured in the flesh, people think that they have a disease. They feel sick.

But both the psychic fixation and the physical picture are nothing. Both are entirely unreal. The healer only needs to know the Truth. Never let yourself be led into handling the flesh with your thought by visualizing a perfect organism, for that is hypnotic, and therefore a harmful influence.  Ignore the body, and give your mind to the Holy Spirit.

There are some schools of healing which teach their students to deny the organ.  I know a woman who denied a kidney out of existence, when she was having trouble with it. She destroyed her kidney.  That was not a healing; it was a psychic operation which she performed upon herself.

You do not need to deny a fleshly condition — except momentarily, if someone has tried to impress you with the condition, and you say to yourself that there is no such thing, and turn away from it.  You realize the Truth of God, and you keep knowing that in God these things do not obtain. There is no cause or force or power operative that would produce such a thing as disease in man.

If you are called upon to heal a seeming drunkard, you may know that there is no desire in man for strong drink. One reason why there is no desire for strong drink is that there is no strong drink.   Man made that belief, but it has no power.  If you believe in strong drink, you are, so to speak, giving power to a material substance, when the Spirit of God is the only Substance and the only Power.  Men have been so psychologized through the centuries that they have taken on all sorts of psychic fixations.  We name these fixations and call some of the "strong drink," or "narcotics." We give them a pseudo-power, and then we bow down to the power we have given them.

"Abide in Me," said Jesus.  "If ye abide in Me, and My words abide in you, ye shall ask what ye will, and it shall be done unto you."  "The words that I speak unto you, they are spirit, and they are life." We must abide in the Truth and not allow ourselves to be drawn into the untruth. We must keep our eye single and not allow ourselves to be disturbed by any evil that we see or hear. So many people are disturbed. They work themselves into a mental fever over some horrible crime they have read about, and they feel as if they would like to go out and shoot that man. "He isn't fit to live," they say. They get angry and upset over what men do and the state the world is in. Then they wonder why *they* get into a state of illness. Their state is the result of their own agitation, their belief in the reality of this non-good.

Many sicknesses are brought about because people allow themselves to descend into such states of consciousness, and wallow in them. If anybody wants to go to hell, he only needs to read the morning papers, and then he can be right in the midst of it quite easily. But that hell-state of consciousness is a delusion of bondage and tyranny and suffering and want, which sometimes nearly destroys the one who indulges in it and feeds upon it.

The attention of most people is turned in the wrong direction. They are entertaining the wrong kind of thoughts and feelings. For man is spiritual. His desires are spiritual, and he is not really interested in non-realities. He wants the Truth, and he is always being instructed in the Truth, though he passes it by without hearing it. If he would turn in the *right* direction, to God alone, he would receive the Divine Instruction of the Infinite Wisdom. His perception, his understanding, his whole being, would be filled by the Holy Spirit.

That is the instruction man wants. He really wants the things of the Spirit. He desires and craves inner things. He often misinterprets that craving, and therefore makes the mistake of seeking outwardly and trying to satisfy his hunger with outer things. He does not realize that he already *is* all that he wants to be, and that the *things* he wants are now present in all their perfection. The only trouble with man is that he does not *know* that God's Kingdom is now within him in all its fullness. He does not *know* that the Power and the Glory of the Divine are here, and that all now lives and moves and has its being in God.

This is the Truth, but to know it requires steadfastness. We must abide in the Truth in order to know it. And we must stand firm in the face of those things which challenge the mind with anything other than the Truth. If we can fully and deeply know the Truth, the Truth will eventually set us free.

But we are not abiding in the Truth if we get disturbed over something and feel badly and say, "Oh dear! Why is it so?" It is not so, and we must be steadfast in knowing that it is not so. It *seems* so. The seeming may be pronounced, but it is all in the seeming. Lazarus seemed to be dead. He had been buried four days. That was a pretty strong seeming. But Jesus knew that Lazarus was not dead.

The "seemings" are not true, no matter how strong they appear. When we realize the Truth fully in our own consciousness, we shall be able to dislodge and dispel that fog of misconceptions which we call the human mind, and free the individual. When anyone is freed through the clear, complete understanding of the Truth, he is freed for all time. He will not return to that bondage in this life, or the so-called life to come. It will be finished completely.

You need to know, in every case you have, that the work is finished, complete. Sometimes, perhaps, you have treated, and then you hope and wonder. But if you know that there is nothing but God, and that there was nothing to heal, you can rise to that state of consciousness whereby you can see the finished fact — that it is done — and there will be no return ever.

It will not be that you have done anything yourself, except that you have known the Truth. The Truth, being recognized, acts *apparently;* and the freeing takes place. The Truth makes free; and when you know that, you take no credit to yourself for having done anything. You forget the case. It is finished. It is gone. It was simply nothing anyway; so you do not turn back to it or think about it. You do not want credit or personal satisfaction — if you are "a healer."

# LESSON VIII

SPIRITUAL healing is a ministry, and as such it demands consecration. It appoints us to self-surrender. We have to abandon all self-interest and lay aside the personality through which we ordinarily think and desire and imagine. We are called to a pure, impersonal vision of Truth, to a disinterested and selfless life of service.

We have to be free of self, that is, of the mortal or personal self. We have to become empty of all things that would tend to interfere or block the action of the Spirit in us. We have to let go of our own will and entirely forsake this outer mind of ours, which disquiets us with its ambitions and restlessness and disappointments and dissatisfactions.

This is one of the steps to bliss, or peace, that Gautama Buddha spoke of. He said that we could not enter into bliss unless we had taken certain steps, and that one of them was the dropping of the mind.

Jesus emphasized this renunciation throughout all His teaching. "I came, . . . not to do Mine own will, but the Will of Him that sent Me," He said. And He made it plain that "whosoever shall not receive the Kingdom of God as a little child shall in no wise enter therein."

The Apostle Paul speaks of this mind that exercises itself with the outer world as "the carnal mind." He says: "To be carnally minded is death; but to be spiritually minded is life and peace. Because the carnal mind is enmity against God: for it is not subject to the Law of God, neither indeed can be." It goes its own way, full of anxiety and eagerness for place and station, and occupied with its own desire to grasp and to have and to hold. It is quite unlike, and indeed is opposed to, the Mind of God.

If we are really at all in the ministry of healing, we willingly drop this self-mind — which is not mind, but is a turning of our power of love toward our own person. It is a state of consciousness which is ignorance and death.

But we are called to know the Divine Mind, the Divine Life. All are called who are to any degree conscious of the meaning of the Name of Christ, and have taken upon themselves to follow after Him.

The Scriptures say: "Many are called, but few are chosen." This is because many do not catch the word of His high calling; or, if they hear it, they are not willing to give their hearts to the understanding of it. No one can recognize the call of the Holy Spirit when his heart is full of selfishness and greed and competition and restlessness. Nor can anyone respond to that call except by rising above himself toward the Peace of the One in whose service he is called.

The healer must be at peace. He must know — to some degree, at least — what the Great Peace is. He must be more aware of that "peace of God, which passeth all understanding," than he is of anything that goes on around him. He must be able to stand in the midst of turmoil and keep serene, poised, and unperturbed, though everybody else may be caught in the conditions that are bred of struggle and strife. He must be so wholly centered in the One and Only

Mind, the Perfect Peace of God, that he can say, as did Paul, "None of these things move me."

Disturbing reports came to Paul in regard to the Corinthian church — how the members were behaving, with bickerings and jealousies and resentments and strife, accusing one another and contending one against the other for place and recognition. It seemed as though all his teaching and his work with them had been in vain.

But Paul had already "determined not to know anything among you, save Jesus Christ." So he was not at all harassed or discouraged, but, on the contrary, he made of their dissensions an opportunity for Love Itself to express many mighty things of the Spirit through him, for the good of all the world. Thus he moved not away from the Love and the Peace and the Power of God, but continued to speak the word of Truth, "which the Holy Ghost teacheth."

We must be established in that clear, untroubled state of mind if we would heal as vehicles of the Holy Spirit. We must have the harmony of peace and joy and love and kindliness and good will. These are what constitute health and wholeness. These are what constitute the consciousness of the spiritual healer.

Our consciousness must be free from strife and struggle and strain. Most diseases come from these three things: the strife among men, the struggle of competition and rivalry, the strain of trying to get those things which are temporal and which, when obtained, can give no contentment, no health or life or love. They are not real. Nothing temporal is real. He who labors for "the meat which perisheth" is habitually in a state of dissatisfaction, unrest, and fear of loss.

But he who would heal must be habitually in the Kingdom of God, the Kingdom of Reality. He must walk in that Kingdom. It is his place of abode, his habitation, wherein he abides with the things of the Spirit. He must keep his mind above externals. He must know, absolutely *know*, that man is not a physical or material being. He must be entirely free from the idea that the body is the self. He must truly know that "the flesh profiteth nothing," that it has no power, no intelligence, and no will, but is "as the grass." And he must turn within to the Spirit, that he may learn more and more of the Spirit and come to know the Real Self within him. For to know that Divine Self is to know all that is.

This learning and this knowing require discipline of the outer mind and personal self. The healer must discipline himself. The art of healing comes only by discipline and obedience. Some people think that it is easy to be a healer. But the Cross is not easy, and the way of the healer is the way of the Cross.

There must be the crossing out of self — the rejection of all self-ambition, self-satisfaction, and self-success. Even the *desire* for personal recognition and praise and deference must be set aside. "If any man will come after Me, let him deny himself, and take up his cross, and follow Me." We put away ambition and worry and effort to shine. We drop our natural will and desire to be healers, and cease to serve or profit our personal selves in any way whatever.

"I came, . . . not to do Mine own will, but the Will of Him that sent Me."

Those who would enter the ministry of healing have to follow the Christ. "I am the Way," He said. Not, "You are the way"; but, "I am the Way." If you are called to the mintry, you are called to the dropping of your will and the letting go of self, that the Divine may use you.

We have to be willing to drop all that we have and all that we seem to be. We are to become empty vessels; and we have to let go of all wishes in order to become vessels for God's Word — empty, and as nothing of ourselves.

Jesus did not say that it is an easy way to travel. He said, "Strait is the gate, and narrow is the way, which leadeth unto life, and few there be that find it." Yet He said also, "My yoke is easy, and My burden is light." His *yoke* is easy, but not His way. His way is one of entire self-surrender, of losing your life, of denying your own will.

But by following His way, which seems so difficult, you receive His yoke and are joined to His Presence of "all power . . . in heaven and in earth." It is then that you become strong with that Strength which has overcome the world and are enabled to do with ease those things which formerly were hard. "With God all things are possible," every step of the way.

But we have to train for the ministry. We have to be set apart, just as an athlete is set apart in training for the race he is to run, or the game he is to play.

An athlete has to obey the rules of the training master. He has to avoid extremes. He has to regulate his activities into certain hours and definite purposes. He has to eat at the training table, and he is not given the alluring delicacies that appeal to the taste, but must eat foods that are essential, nourishing, and non-fattening. He must not waste his breath or his steadiness; so he cannot smoke or drink. He is not allowed any pleasures of his own, nor can he indulge in any gaieties or any laziness just .to please others. He must be strong, mentally and physically. He must train, with his eye on the goal.

It is a sacrifice to be an athlete. It is a sacrifice to be a musician or a painter or a writer or a scientist. And it is a sacrifice to be a healer.

He who would be strong in the things of the Spirit must take the training of the Spirit. He cannot be spending his life purposelessly. He cannot be frittering away his time with things that simply pamper the senses. He cannot be engaged in silliness and foolishness, though all around him people may be thus engaged.

It is not that he condemns anything — that is, in the way we use the word *condemn*. In another way, however, he does condemn, because to "condemn" means to render useless, or to know a thing to be of no use. When a building, for instance, has served its purpose and is no longer usable, it is *condemned*, or pronounced useless.

There are many things that must be condemned by him who walks in the narrow path, for he will see the uselessness of them. He will be set apart, so that he may not expend his energies upon those things which are of no use and no benefit to him in his ministry of service. He must be free of futile and profitless thoughts and activities. He must drop them out of his life.

Those who want these things can have them. The All-

Good gives us anything we want. As Emerson expressed it, "What will you have? quoth God; pay for it and take it." We always pay for everything we get. The people who want dreams and foolishness get just that and pay for their self-indulgence with their lives.

If we want to have the consciousness of Christ and to work the works of the Spirit, we must and do pay highly for it. We also pay with our life, with the attention and devotion and consecration of our whole heart. But says the Christ, "Him that cometh to Me I will in no wise cast out." "Whosoever will lose his life for My sake shall find it."

He who would heal must be of one mind, with one purpose — single-eyed, one-pointed, steadfast. He must keep his eye on the mark of the high calling unto which he has been called. He can never drift, nor yield himself to be drawn away into side issues which may seem important to other people. For there is a constant pull toward the outer world, and there are plenty of people who seem to be set on turning him aside.

But he who would succeed must listen only to the Voice of the Holy Spirit. He must forsake *all,* and follow Christ. "But this one thing I do," said Paul, "forgetting those things which are behind, . . . I press toward the mark for the prize of the high calling of God in Christ Jesus."

The healer clings to that one thing, devotes himself to that one thing. And that one thing that he does is to acquaint himself with the Reality of Being, and to know that God is All.

Many people believe in God, but few people *know* God. Many people attend religious services and ceremonies, have religious longings and spiritual uplifts, and pray to God every day. But this does not mean that they know God. Only the few know and understand that God is real — actual. The many believe that there must be such a Being, but they are not conscious of that Being. They do not feel the touch of the Infinite, and they do not hear the Voice of the Eternal. To them the Voice is silent; it is far away.

The Voice of God has been called "the still small Voice," and it is indeed inaudible; yet it can be heard. The Divine Reality can be known, the Divine Presence can be felt. If we feel after God with all our heart and mind and soul, we shall find Him. We shall hear Him and know Him, and experience Him in our consciousness as the Only Real and Actual One.

The healer is ever on the alert to the Spirit, on the watch for the things of the Spirit. He is ever sensing and acknowledging the Divine Presence. He walks in the Peace of God and knows the Love of God which brings strength and joy. He feels the inner Joy of the Spirit, that Joy which no man can take away.

Those who find their happiness in some pleasant occurrence will find sorrow and disappointment in unpleasant occurrences. If their joy comes to them from the words or acts of some friend, this joy will be gone when the friend does or says something to the contrary. Such happiness is temporal; it is not real and can be easily disrupted and destroyed. It is misleading. The healer must have that Joy which no one and nothing can hurt. The Joy of the Spirit is not affected by anything that is said or done personally whether pleasant or unpleasant.

There are those who are easily disturbed by what others do or say or think about them. They are sensitive and pride themselves on their sensitiveness. The healer cannot be that way. To be easily hurt is a sign of being wrapped up in self-will. To be disturbed by externals is to be walking in self-ishness. It is only self-esteem that makes anyone sensitive toward other people and what they say about him.

There is a sensitiveness, however, which is open only to God and feels only His Spirit. It is not touched at all by externals. It is wholly indifferent to the thoughts and judg-ments of men. This sensitiveness is a consciousness which is so fine and pure and acutely responsive to the Divine that it feels the zephyrs of the Heavenly Realm and perceives the silent Word of the Spirit.

That is a different kind of sensitiveness. It is the aware-ness of God that arises in us when the untrue self is put away — when we are willing to dismiss out of our hearts all desire for personal gain and to be washed clean of all those things that are not of the Spirit.

Then we become truly sensitive to the Kingdom of God and to all that obtains in His Kingdom. It is then that the inner ear opens, which enables us to hear the Voice of the Spirit. With that new hearing we are alive to the whisper-ings of the Silence, and we catch the word that is healing.

This takes training. It requires meditation and concen-tration. But, as you doubtlessly know, you cannot concen-trate unless you love. Back of all the thought-wanderings and difficulties in concentration is simply the lack of love, for it is easy to keep your attention on that which you love.

Jesus said that the first commandment is to love God

with all your heart and mind and soul. If there is the love of God in the heart, it is not a duty, but a joy, to concentrate on the things of the Spirit. But if we are in love with ourselves rather than with God, we shall think of ourselves rather than God.

There have always been those — and there are many today — who turn to God, not because of their love for Him, but because of what they want and think they can get from Him. Of course, they deceive themselves, for they are not turning to God. What they turn to is but a figurehead, a lifeless image. The living, loving God finds no open heart in them, through which He can pour His blessings out upon mankind. Such people are full of themselves, and so busy with their own plans and desires and prayers for something that they know not the way to receive.

Jesus said that the way to get is to give, and that the way to have it to let go and not have. "He that loveth his life shall lose it." "He that loseth his life for My sake (in love for God) shall find it."

For man's life is in God and of God, the One and the All; and if man seeks a separate life of his own, he must of course lose it, because such a thing does not exist. The statements of Truth seem paradoxical because of the Oneness and Allness of God. There is no life in man save that of the Holy Spirit. When anyone understands the Truth, all its seemingly contradictory statements cohere into the saying of one thing: GOD IS ALL.

The Truth says:

"Everyone that exalteth himself shall be abased; and he that humbleth himself shall be exalted."

"Many that are first shall be last; and the last shall be first."

"Sell that thou hast, and give."

"Whosoever hath, to him shall be given."

To the man of reason these, and many other such statements, seem like self-contradictory foolishness. But the Truth does not contradict; only its word is two-edged.

The Truth stands, we might say, as our adversary and our friend. It is the adversary of our mortal mind and the friend of our spiritual understanding. The Spirit of Truth opposes, or makes null and void, all mortal activities — not by acting against these false and seeming activities, for they are nothingness, but simply by being all there *is*.

Because God is all there is, it follows that as we lose our darkness, we find His Light. There was nothing but Light all the time. As we walk away from the flesh, or mortal mind, we find that we are moving into the Presence of Reality. There was never any other presence but Reality. And so, as we lay aside our personal selves, we find the Divine Self — which was always the only Self. "If any man will come after Me, let him deny himself, . . . and follow He," said Jesus. That is the way out of our delusions. That is the way to the Truth which sets us free.

The soul ceases to strive when it finds the Self. It lets go of everything. It abandons itself to That One, and opens itself to the Divine Inspiration. When our *desire* for externals is gone, we no longer seek for anything external. We live in the Spirit and forget things. Then we find that all things are given to us from the Source, from the Giver of all good things.

If we would be healers, we do not strain ourselves with our desire for things, for results, for appearances. We do just the opposite. We abandon them; we let go of them. We empty ourselves; and in emptying ourselves, we find that we are filled with the Truth.

As we humble ourselves before the High I Am, the Omnipotent and Omniscient One, we find ourselves partaking of His Omnipotence and Omniscience. As we let go of the wisdom of this world, we find ourselves being instructed in the Heavenly Wisdom. When we bow down to the Infinite, we are God-taught. The Divine then teaches us the ways of righteousness. He leads our feet in the paths of peace. We are guided out of lack and want, and are given all things needful. We are carried along in our work and prospered and cared for.

It is the same way with our desire for power — the power to heal. There are many who seek that power. But if we would have it, we must forsake the seeking for it. We must not want a powerful mind and a strong will. We must let go of mind and will.

Jesus said, "Seek, and ye shall find." But when we are seeking for power, we are seeking our own power; and, you remember, He said, "I can of Mine own self do nothing." So we abandon ourselves to the One Supreme, and abide in Him.

Then, having become free from the self-desire for power, we find His power. Having put aside all ambition for glory, we are bathed in the Glory of the Infinite. Seeking only the Eternal and not wanting to shine of ourselves, we become luminous with the Light of God shining through us.

There are many who want to heal, but who are not successful in their work. It is because their minds are so filled with plans and methods and anxieties that the things of this world absorb their consciousness. The thoughts of the world are part of them.

The minds that are filled with outer things are not fit channels for the flowing of the Holy Expression. If we would heal, we must be free from anxieties and worry and fear. We must have a serenity and confidence that nothing can disturb.

To be successful healers, we must be transformed into selflessness; for serenity, fearlessness, and confidence arise only out of selflessness. But we do not try to transform ourselves. We deny ourselves. We withdraw from ourselves and commit our minds to be renewed with the Spirit. Then we are transformed by the Eternal One.

If we give our minds and hearts to be trained by the Eternal, we shall know that Self which is without variableness. It will hold us high and keep us steady and wise and strong in the midst of the turmoil and strife of the world.

Though we seem to have to do with sickness and suffering and all sorts of wretchedness, we shall have nothing to do with them. These things shall not move us nor touch us nor enter into our hearts to disturb us.

For if we are truly walking in the consciousness of the Eternal, there will be the All-knowing Love working through us and freeing those who are in bondage to the temporal and the false. They will be lifted out of their trouble by the heavenly grace which flows through our consciousness of God's Invariableness and Omniscience and Omnipotence.

As we are more and more conscious of the Eternal Love, we are more and more lifted, sustained, and inspirited with the *grace* of the Infinite. He that walks under grace is free from the law. He no longer has to consider the law when he is in the Spirit.

"For the law was given by Moses, but grace and truth came by Jesus Christ." He who walks with Christ walks under grace; he walks conscious of the Life of the Spirit, and is therefore able to free those who are still under bondage to the law.

There are those who say that it is wrong to heal spiritually because this unmerited release from bondage is an interference with the law of karma — of cause and effect. These people do not know the Love of God, which is the Law of Grace. They do not understand the meaning of the Divine Forgiveness. These are still under their belief in the law given by Moses. They are still hearing it said, "An eye for an eye, and a tooth for a tooth."

Moses gave his people the law of karma. But when Jesus Christ came, He spoke thus: "Moses told you this, and Moses told you that, but I tell you something else. I say unto you: 'God loves you unchangeably, whether you merit His Love or not. This is grace and truth. You need only recognize it and know it and respond to it — and you will be free.' "

Jesus Christ was Himself an interference to the law of karma. He interfered so completely that He broke down the power of that law.

"There is therefore now no condemnation to them which are in Christ Jesus, who walk not after the flesh, but after the Spirit."

"But God, who is rich in mercy, for His great Love wherewith He loved us, even when we were dead in sins, hath quickened us together with Christ. . . . For by grace are ye saved through faith; and that not of yourselves: it is the gift 'of God."

"Son, be of good cheer, thy sins be forgiven thee" is the speech of Jesus Christ. And when the scribes, just as they do today, thought within themselves that the law was being blasphemed, Jesus said: "Wherefore think ye evil in your hearts? For whether is easier, to say, Thy sins be forgiven thee; or to say, Arise, and walk?"

"God is Love." "Arise, and walk." "Neither hath this man sinned, nor his parents." "I bring you good tidings of great joy," that the Glory of God may be manifest in you! This is the Christ Message and the revelation of the Holy Spirit which is in the heart of the true healer.

But if the healer is not walking under grace, he will become tangled in karmic thought. He will get into trouble also, because he will not have come into that freedom which is of Christ; and so he will not be strong enough to meet karmic conditions. He will not have the forgiveness that is in the Truth, nor will he have really felt that "the law of the Spirit of life in Christ Jesus hath made me free from the law of sin and death." Not being free in his own consciousness, he will not be able to dissolve those effects which are brought about by habitual sin and persistent error.

The healer must abandon all externals — for the karmic law is external to the Spirit — and he must rise with Christ above the law. Then he will be able to set others free from the law.

Thus the healer is one who sets others free by reason of his consciousness of the grace of God. He walks in that grace, in the Spirit of Christ, being led by the Spirit of God. Therefore he is not walking under the law, but transcends the law in his consciousness of the Allness of the Divine and the nothingness of aught other. With his eye single to the Divine Wholeness and his tongue tipped with the celestial instinction that comes from the knowing of the Truth in Christ, he shall catch the word of the Spirit and shall speak it.

Then those who are sitting in darkness shall open their eyes and behold the Light. Those who are in pain shall feel the Peace of God. Those who are in sickness and disease shall rise up out of them, for these falsities will fall away and disappear into nothingness. They are not part of the heavenly grace. They have no place in the Kingdom of God.

The healer must be unceasingly training himself to walk in that Kingdom. You know that the athlete must keep up his training and must not slacken in his obedience. The athlete must keep his purpose in mind and act accordingly. He must comply with and follow the directions given him in order to accomplish that which he has undertaken to do. If he has not been strict with himself, he will be weak and untrustworthy in his game.

So, also, it is with the spiritual athlete. He must not be diverted by outer claims or pursuits. He must keep his mind on God. "Thou wilt keep him in perfect peace, whose mind is stayed on thee."

When you enter into the healing ministry, you are in the most difficult business in all the world. You are in the most exacting profession there is. And your work is the most dangerous in all the universe. The path is not a path of roses, but is so narrow that there is no room in it for yourself at all. Since you can do nothing of yourself, it is dangerous for you to think you can. I might say that it is dangerous for you to think at all when treating. You have to let be what *is*, and you have to *know* what is. You have to do this all the time and be ready every moment. Christ told us not to think, but to watch and pray. "And what I say unto you, I say unto all, Watch."

You cannot watch the One unless you give up every thought, every desire, every purpose of your own. You cannot endure "as seeing Him who is invisible," unless you have become so blind and deaf to the visible, personal world that you do not feel its existence. There must be nothing in you which can distract or divert your attention away from the Invisible and Unconquerable One. You must be single-eyed and one-pointed in mind.

Notwithstanding all the promises and unutterable rewards of the Spirit, it is not easy to die to yourself voluntarily so that you may know God, the Reality. But that is what is required of the spiritual healer. Every desire, wish, want, will, and concern for self must go, and be as naught, that Christ may be All in all, that you may "put on Christ," that you may "let Christ be formed in you." For without Christ you can do nothing; and with Him you can do all.

Some practitioners attempt to heal with affirmations and denials according to Truth. They do this with good intention, but their word is sent forth from their own minds. They work hard and quite sincerely, and then they wonder why it is all to no effect. It is because they do not *know* Him in whom they believe.

Words of themselves do not heal. It is the realization of God in your very heart's blood that draws the Power of the Spirit into your ministry. Otherwise there is no substance in what you say, and your word is lifeless. It has no potency.

"Without Me (without the Dynamic Spirit, the Deific Essence) ye can do nothing." But when the word is charged with the dynamic of the Spirit of God, it goes forth and accomplishes that whereunto it is sent.

Your healing is successful because of the Divine quality and essence in your word — not because you speak it. Indeed, you cannot really speak it until you have realized the Presence of Him who has given it to you for others.

To heal is to lose one's life for the lives of others. But you lose your life, not in their lives, but in the Life of Christ. He who is willing to do that finds that the Spirit works with him and through him, and is always ready to do the Father's good pleasure by his word.

It is the Father's good pleasure to give man the Kingdom of Heaven, to restore him to peace and health and wholeness, and to make him walk upright again in the glory of his sonship.

The Christ healing awakens man out of his lethargy. It arouses and quickens him that he may stand up and walk in the glory of his sonship to the Supreme. Christ does not pay any attention to the flesh, nor to those things with which the flesh has been affected through error and falsity.

Likewise the spiritual healer, abandoning himself to the Christ Mind, concerns himself only with the Truth, the pure Truth which is God. He devotes himself to the Divine Principle of Life. He seeks God, and God only. He opens himself to the Divine and closes himself to all else. "And ye shall seek Me, and find Me, when ye shall search for Me with all your heart."

This seeking is not done by any stretching of the thoughts of the mind. It is not an effort of the will nor a straining of the soul. It is by meekness and lowliness and simplicity of heart that we seek and find God. For, as a wise mystic has said, "By love may He be gotten and holden, but by thought never."

When Christ stands at the door and knocks, it is the intent of the heart that He sees; and it is the open, cloudless mind that He enters. Whosoever truly loves the Christ, to him will He truly come, and abide in his heart and in his consciousness. And wherein Christ abides is the Kingdom of God manifested.

When we submit ourselves to Christ in singleness of heart, devotedness to service, and with no desire save to do good toward others, we shall feel the inspiration and the quickening and the teaching of the Spirit in the things of the Kingdom. We shall feel and know the mysteries of the Kingdom; and in that knowing of the Light, we shall quicken others to seek the Truth. Then they will respond and turn from their delusions, and shall also walk in the Light.

"Return unto Me, and I will return unto you, saith the Lord of Hosts." When we shall acquaint ourselves with the Divine Sonship within us and know our Christhood, we shall know all things and fear nothing.

Sometimes people say, "I have tried and tried, but I don't seem to get anywhere." We do not have to get anywhere. We do not have to strive to progress. We do not have to labor and work to do good. Our only work is to enter into that *rest* which is the Kingdom of God. For all that the Father has belongs to the Son. The healer must always be at rest. He who walks in the Spirit is always at rest.

We have an illustration of this rest in mechanics. For instance, when a wheel is perfectly poised on its bearings, there is a place, an infinitesimal point at its center, which is always absolutely still, no matter how fast the wheel revolves.

Thus God has been described by the mystic as "the Infinitesimal Point." That which is at rest within us is the Invisible God-Point. We turn to that God-Point and find rest.

The Kingdom of God is in the Inmost of our being. That does not mean in the stomach or liver or solar plexus or any physical organ. It means in the I AM, in our spiritual Being.

When you know that Secret Place, that Infinitesimal Point within you, you know that Center of Being which is immovable and invariable, and which cannot ever be touched or disturbed or hurt. Neither can you be disturbed or hurt when you are walking in the consciousness of that perfect rest which is the Kingdom of God.

When you are consciously living in that Realm from

which the flowing of the Spirit emerges, you will know the wellspring of Life and drink of the living waters which the Christ gives to them who are with Him in Spirit and in Truth.

Your word will then be alive with that potency, that dynamic, that essence, which is of the Kingdom of God and comes by the free action of the Spirit of grace. The Kingdom of God is within you, but now you are aware that it is within you; you know it, and you *know* that you know.

You are not afraid of any condition, any man, any circumstance. Fear is something that has departed from your consciousness. You are indifferent to all these outer things. God has been called "the Great Indifferent" by the ancient mystics. When we acquaint ourselves with Him, we shall partake of that great indifference; and we shall not lose our heads over any conditions, no matter how obstinate and exasperating they may be. Walking on the heights with the Eternal, the Absolute One, we shall not be moved.

In that divine indifference, which is the wisdom and the freedom and the compassion of Christ, we find that all things are ours, and that our work is unlabored. This does not mean that we shall not have difficult things to do; "for unto whomsoever much is given, of him shall be much required."

Much that we do will seem difficult, if not impossible, to the eyes of mortals. But we shall do with ease those things that are indeed too hard for us, because we shall not do them of ourselves. They will be done through us by the grace of God, while we are but vehicles for His Omnipotence and

Omniscience. "Behold, I am the Lord, the God of all flesh: is there any thing too hard for Me?"

As we behold Him, our mind is illuminated with the wisdom that is from above, and the Holy Spirit quietly pours out upon us that knowledge and power which the outer man strives for and cannot get. It is done within.

He who would heal must not allow his mind to go the way of the outer man. He must keep himself training in the Way of the Spirit. He surrenders himself to that one purpose, with his heart's attention ever lifted to the Most High.

Then, like the athlete who can go out and represent his school, the healer can go out and represent the Spirit and show the ways of the Spirit to mankind. Having become conscious of his oneness with the One, he knows his real Self and walks eternally with the Spirit of God, free and glad and strong — not of himself, but because God is free and glad and strong.

The work of the healer becomes effortless because of the Divine Strength that possesses him and moves out from within him. "I can of Mine own self do nothing," said Jesus.

If the healer thinks that he himself can do anything at all, he must overcome that idea. He cannot do it. "I am not come of Myself. . . . I do nothing of Myself. . . . I speak not of Myself: but the Father that dwelleth in Me, He doeth the works."

Our work is to forget ourselves and remember the Father, the Supreme. In Him is rest and light and joy. As we are faithful in our forgetfulness of self and our remembrance of Him, we shall be led more and more toward the concentration of our whole heart in the Spirit. For the power of

loving and knowing the Most High is the gift which God
Himself gives us, by which we may be *conscious* of our oneness with Him who is the I AM THAT I AM.

Acquaint now thyself with Me, and be at peace. Be at
peace with the Divine Self that is within you and within all
your patients. "I will heal their backsliding, I will love them
freely," says the Lord.

If we are acquainted with the One, nothing but good shall
come to us; nothing shall disturb us or make us afraid;
nothing shall injure or hurt us. We shall be immune, untouched. We shall walk freely over the earth, in the world
but not of the world. While the world may be struggling
and striving and stewing, we shall walk serene, poised, untroubled. But we shall not be idle, because the Spirit worketh and worketh, incessantly and constantly.

Whether we are awake or asleep in our conscious mind,
the Spirit will be working in us and through us to will and
to do His good pleasure. We may lay ourselves down in
peace and sleep, for we shall know that the Divine is forever at work. He that watches over the earth shall never
slumber or sleep. He is always awake.

We may know that when we are asleep at night, we may
be at rest, for the Father is still doing the work. When we
understand this, we are never anxious about our cases.
"Take no (anxious) thought," said Jesus. "It is I; be not
afraid." "Let not your heart be troubled."

If you are anxious about your cases, search yourself. You
will discover that you are interested in yourself, your eyes
are on yourself and on your fear that you may fail. But
know this: You can neither succeed nor fail. You cannot do

anything. God is All and in all, and beside Him there is none else.

When a healer is anxious and uncertain about his cases, he has forgotten God and is considering himself. Wondering about results, uneasy about what people may think, and fearing that he may fall down, he does fall down; for his consciousness is engrossed with himself.

We must absolutely *know* that it is the Father that does the work. We must become so thoroughly empty of self that we are not concerned about what we are doing or not doing, and so turned away from self that we never think about whether or not we are representing the Truth.

Some people spend a great deal of their time wondering if they are good representations of the Truth. The Truth will get along quite well without representation. It will stand. When we are concerned and worried like that, our minds are on our own selves. Also, way down in our minds, we are wondering what someone thinks of us. We have to dwell in that order of being in which we are indifferent to what people think.

If we are full of self-importance and false fearing, we are not fit channels through which the Spirit may work. Be anxious about nothing. Walk in the Kingdom of God, which is the Kingdom of Love and Joy and Strength and Peace.

Anxiety always dissipates your energies. If you are anxious about a case, you are frustrating your own purpose and hurting the patient. The first thing that meets us on a case is anxiety on the part of the relatives and friends of the patient, and this is the first thing to be negated and dis-

solved. If you are anxious, you are only adding to their
anxiety and fear.

If your mind were full of the divine realization, there
would not be any room in your heart for anxiety. Be concerned only with the One. Seek the Kingdom of God *first;*
and love the Lord thy God *first.* See to it that you look
only to the Lord, and He will heal your case.

The athlete sees to it that he keeps himself in form. He
is told to "watch his step," and he does. He obeys all the demands and commands put upon him. He brings all his
energies and desires and body into obedience to his one purpose. He surrenders all, that he may fulfill the require-
ments.

That is what we have to do as healers. We are always in
training. We have to surrender all and put our whole attention, might, mind, soul, and strength on the one purpose.
We have to hold to that one purpose and consecrate our
whole being to it. Nothing else counts with us. We have
given ourselves to one thing. "Forgetting those things
which are behind, . . . I press toward the mark for the prize
of the high calling of God in Christ Jesus."

Then we shall be the chosen. Then we shall go forth to
minister. Our joy will be in ministering. We shall be un-
hampered by the thought of getting and wanting things for
ourselves. We shall be free from desire and from need. We
shall be free and joyous in our ministry, and we shall be
abundantly provided for by the Wisdom of God Himself.
We shall know the Divine Joy.

When you have the Divine Joy in your heart which nothing can silence, which no person, no circumstance, no

thought can quench, you will be a good healer. No event that takes place, no sight that meets the eye or noise that strikes the ear, can silence that joy chord which is sounding within you when you are walking in the Kingdom of God with Christ Jesus.

For the real Joy comes from God and not from anything without. It passes understanding, just as His Peace passes understanding. It is Strength. The Divine Joy is Supernal Strength. The Kingdom of God is the Kingdom of Joy, of Peace and Power and Poise and Kindness and Love.

Love is the Supreme. Love is the Eternal. Love fulfills all. If your heart is filled with love for the Eternal, you will also be filled with love for the offspring of the Eternal. You will love to serve; but you will be serving the Divinity in man, not man's aches and pains.

Christ abides with the Divinty in you to guide and bless you in your training. Christ comrades with the Divine Self of man. If we train with God in Christ Jesus, we shall find that we are walking in the Kingdom of the Heights of Glory with Him.

Then we can inspire others to look up rather than down, so that they too may walk freely out of the entanglements in which they have been ensnared. They shall arise out of those conditions that had seemed to fetter and bind them. They too shall come up into understanding, and find peace and poise and joy and strength. They shall shine with the God Radiance, with the Son-shining of righteousness; and they shall know the Kingdom of Heaven, which is the Glory of the God Consciousness.

These words spoke Jesus:

"Neither pray I for these alone, but for them also which shall believe on Me through their word; that they all may be one; as Thou, Father, art in Me, and I in Thee, that they also may be one in Us: that the world may believe that Thou hast sent Me.

"And the glory which Thou gavest Me I have given them; that they may be one, even as We are one: I in them, and Thou in Me, that they may be made perfect in one; and that the world may know that Thou hast sent Me, and hast loved them, as thou hast loved Me."